Clipping Their Own Wings

The Incompatibility between Latino Culture and American Education

Ernesto Caravantes

HAMILTON BOOKS
A member of
The Rowman & Littlefield Publishing Group
Lanham • Boulder • New York • Toronto • Oxford

Copyright © 2006 by
Hamilton Books
4501 Forbes Boulevard
Suite 200
Lanham, Maryland 20706
Hamilton Books Acquisitions Department (301) 459-3366

PO Box 317
Oxford
OX2 9RU, UK

Library of Congress Control Number: 2006927173
ISBN-13: 978-0-7618-3536-3 (paperback : alk. paper)
ISBN-10: 0-7618-3536-9 (paperback : alk. paper)

This book is respectfully dedicated to all the brave men and women who have perished in the attempt to create a better life for their families by immigrating to the United States.

Their loyal dedication to America and her Ideals should be an example for all of us to follow.

Author's Note

The terms *Hispanic* and *Latino* are used interchangeably throughout this book. They are used to denote the peoples of all Latin American heritages living within the borders of the United States, as well as those living within Latin American nations.

There is no assumption that one term is preferable to the other, or that either term connotes superiority. Nor is either given any sociopolitical connotation. They are both given equal weight and used together so as to avoid unnecessary repetition throughout the text.

Contents

Preface

One sunny morning in early 1999, I rode in a taxi through the dusty, congested streets of downtown Lima, Peru. I was winding my way back to the international airport to catch my scheduled flight back to Los Angeles. I had been on a two-week expedition to see the major sites in Peru, such as the Inca mountain fortress of Machu Pichu, the colonial city and former Incan capital Cuzco, and the steamy Amazon rainforest. It was a fascinating trip. However, fourteen days and a strong cold virus later, I was ready to go home. Little did I know that I was about to embark on a far different journey upon my return to California.

As I looked out through the window of the taxi at the streets of Lima, I saw young children playing in the streets and in the neighborhoods. They displayed an innocence that is rare in modern children. They were enjoying simple games. They seemed blissfully unaware of the problems that plague the planet, as children should be. After I came home, I remembered those children and compared them with American children of their same age. My mother remarked how fortunate those Peruvian children are to have such innocence sustained over many years. True, I thought to myself. However, my next thought was: What about when those children grow up? They won't be children forever. I told her this and she agreed. Those little children in Peru may have carefree years when they are young, but they grow up with very few educational and occupational prospects.

I contrasted that situation with the one in the United States. Children in America are afforded fewer years of innocence as the images of violence in video games and television and movies quickly fill their psyches. However, when they grow up, young adults in the United States will have the opportunity to attend some of the best institutions of higher education in the world. The job market also offers careers that could never be offered in a place like Lima.

Ironically, for Latinos in the affluent United States, life is as dismal and ab-ject as it is for many in a city like Lima, Peru. The reason is that they come to America with a low level of education. Increasingly, the minority popula-tion most likely to live in this condition in the United States is Latinos. For many, the migration to the United States became a daring journey in hopes of a better life. Yet, the Latino population has found that it has not been able to attain the prosperity of other immigrant populations, such as Asians. What can account for the difference?

Since even before I had left for my Peruvian adventure, I would now and then visit a young Latin American girl of about 18 who used to work at Olvera Street, the quaint Mexican colonial market in downtown Los Angeles. She was beautiful. Light brown hair, pale skin, small thin face, skinny frame, and the most innocent pair of eyes I have ever seen. She was an absolute angel. I, of course, was quite taken with her, but she already had a boyfriend. So, she and I just maintained casual contact. Then, over the next two years, I found out that she became a mother, still unwed, and had quit her job. She had shown such promise and had appeared so bright. She was even ready to be-gin taking courses at the local community college at the time she and I first met. Now, of course, as a teenage mother, her life would be changed forever. We lost touch with each other over time. She quite her job at Olvera Street, and I never saw her again.

This young girl had all the opportunities open to her. Los Angeles hosts several good universities. UCLA is world-class. Why did she do it? Why did she allow herself to get pregnant? There are so many ways now that a girl and boy can prevent a pregnancy. There are other, countless teenage Latinas who end up in the same predicament. Furthermore, there are countless teenage Latino males who also end up on the wrong side of the tracks. All of this leads to a life of poverty and crime. The sheer irony is that this is happening in the most affluent country in the world. This is happening in a country where there are so many ways to advance oneself through education. But something more is happening here than meets the eye.

Latinos are falling behind other ethnic groups in education, and this sub-sequently affects their future career and occupational prospects. Of course, one can look at the California state budget and blame the problem of Hispanic underachievement on the lack of monies in the legislative coffers. Or, the temptation can be to point to inadequate or overcrowded classrooms as the root cause. One can blame it on society and say that discrimination is at work, always a handy maneuver. Yet, perhaps no one has thought to look at the Latino culture itself as the culprit. Perhaps the Latino culture is the final ar-biter between success and failure. What do I mean by that statement? Aren't there many successful Latinos on television working as anchormen and an-

chorwomen? How did they do it? Aren't there successful Hispanics in education, science, and government in the United States? Yes, thank God. However,
what has helped them most, as I know it did for me, was to successfully navigate between what are essentially two very different cultures. I am convinced
that what will bolster Latinos in their journey towards success in the United
States, more than anything else, will be to incorporate that which is adaptive
from the Anglo-Saxon culture, and yet still retain the beautiful elements of
their native Latino culture. Hispanics have to be judicious in what they select
in the Anglo-Saxon culture, and what they can safely reject. The same process
has to occur in the careful selection of the adoption of key elements of Latino
culture. I coined this term of cultural duality *Selective Cultural Adoption.*

I invented this term to denote that, as in so many areas of life, one must
steer a middle ground. There are those on the right who feel that if only every
immigrant would just assimilate and integrate him or herself, everything will
be fine. I disagree. Furthermore, there are those on the left who want to turn
this country into a United Nations and feel that we should be made aware of
each other's cultures and come to appreciate and celebrate these cultural differences, like it or not. The "force-feed" multicultural approach. I am not entirely inclined to agree with that approach either. I wanted to look closer and
deeper and say that both approaches are short-sided and ultimately wrong. It
is not that Latinos should *just* assimilate or *just* be multicultural. All minority
groups should be in touch with their roots but at the same time, realize that
there may be elements of their roots that may not be working in their best interests to retain, *while living in the United States.* On the other hand, I do not
believe in wholesale adoption of the entire American cultural landscape either. The American media glorifies a culture of violence that I despise. There
is a fierce attempt on the part of corporate America to try and sell cars, gadg-
ets, and other items that really do not go that far in making people any happier and only drive them deeper into debt. It only causes people to feel that
they have to "keep-up-with-the-Joneses." So, what is the answer? Selective
Cultural Adoption. This means that one freely picks the best that one's native
culture has to offer and the best that the American culture has to offer. Some
groups do this without too much effort. It is natural for them. However, for so
many Latinos, the tendency is to retain, lock, stock and barrel, their own native culture and never attempt to adopt anything about the American culture,
not even the English language. They avoid this effort out of sheer mental laziness and fear of sounding inept as they attempt to speak English. So, they
don't even both to try. *Yet, they only shoot themselves in the foot by not even
trying to adopt some very vital elements of American culture.*

This book, however, is not just about culture. Nor does this book solely regard education as its central subject. It goes beyond the scope of either of

those two arenas. This is a book that examines how culture impacts education. I wrote this treatise for anyone who serves and interacts with Latinos students and their families. This is intended to be a critique of ethnic practices and an expose of certain cultural truths. Furthermore, it is written by a Latino who had to struggle very, very hard to get to where he is now.

I believe I may have found the answer that will ultimately explain that which social scientists have been trying to understand for years: Why are Latinos behind in education and not going on to universities at the same rate as other ethnic groups in the United States? Why do they drop out at a higher rate than other ethnic groups? Why is there such a high teen pregnancy rate among Latina adolescent girls? The answer: Latinos, on the whole, have not selectively adopted the elements of the competitive Anglo-Saxon culture that will allow them to succeed in the United States. When they do, other, less acclimated Latinos accuse them of "selling out" to White culture, and discriminate against them. Hispanics can be very insecure, and will want to criticize another Latino who becomes educated and ambitious; it reminds them of their own failure. They will want to pull him or her back down in the mud.

Hispanics in the United States should retain the beauty, the color, vibrancy and spirituality of their native home countries. However, they must adopt the education ethic of the United States. They must adopt the knowledge that in order to advance oneself in the United States, one must attain at least a bachelor's degree. Latinos must aspire to more than the usage of heavily accented conversational English. Their English proficiency must be near perfect if they are to succeed in education as well as the business world. They must set higher expectations for their children's education. In the end, however, I will consider my job done if Hispanics are made more aware of the importance of going to college. Their children's education is in their hands. The time for Latino parents to begin planning to send their children to college is *now*.

This is the age of identity politics. Almost every major ethnic group is clamoring to have its culture recognized and appreciated. At the core of this movement, among Latinos, is the underlying belief that their sense of personal identity will be sacrificed without the constant usage of Spanish in personal conversation at home, the workplace, and even on college campuses. This does not take into account Spanish television, music, and printed material, such as newspapers or books.

Hispanics living in the United States believe that without Spanish they will be stripped of their identity. *What is difficult to grasp is how a language, which is, after all, a medium of communication, can come to ultimately define a human being's complex totality.* For instance, I am a man, a heterosexual, a son, a Christian, a Libertarian, a Taurus, an American, a citizen of California, a native of Long Beach, a resident of Glendale, a college graduate times three, a former cable television talk show host, a bookworm, a very good swimmer, a fast runner, a budding practitioner of the martial arts, and an ex-boyfriend to several young women. I am all of these things. *I am not the English language*. It is merely the language of my country, the United States. It is the commonly agreed upon mode of communicating which my family, my friends, and I all use as residents of this country.

Thus, I have many levels to my personality. The English language is my predominant language; it is the language I speak most often in my day-to-day transactions. Yet, if I suddenly found myself halfway around the world, in a country in which the citizens spoke a non-English language, and I also had to speak their language, I would never, even for a moment, forget who I am or feel that I have now lost my entire sense of self-identity. The many roles that I listed above are always inside me, defining who and what it means to be me. What is more, I *did* find myself living halfway around the world, in a little-known Former Soviet Republic, and I had to learn Romanian, and quick! It was the most difficult and challenging condition under which to learn a new language. I had to practice it daily, and I spoke it often. *However, I was always Ernesto Caravantes. That never changed. My sense of identity was never shaken.*

The argument that Latinos make, in which they state that the Spanish language must be retained and spoken *while living in the United States*, or else they will lose their sense of identity, must be seen for what it is: a lazy man's excuse for not going through the terribly difficult process of learning a new language as an adult. However, Hispanics have it much easier than I ever did when I had to learn Romanian; Latinos are exposed to all sorts of English expressions through the constant bombardment of the American media, cinema, music, books, magazines and television. I was never exposed to Romanian cinema or television shows growing up, thus my process of having to learn Romanian was much more grueling than anything Latinos must do to learn English. The stubborn nature of Hispanic resistance to learn English is only hurting them and alienating them from the rest of the United States. They are causing America to become the Disunited States. Mexicans must stop trying to transform the Southwestern United States into another Mexico. This book will examine the damaging effects of these as well as other cultural blunders that are robbing scores of Latin American elementary students currently living in the United States a precious chance to go to college.

Introduction:
The Nature of the Beast

What if I was to challenge you? What if I told you that something as ordinary as the way a culture views itself in relation to the world is integral to that culture's success or failure? What if I told you that the culture from which you hail will determine, to a greater or lesser extent, how you approach life and its vicissitudes? What if I also told you that you could mold and shape your own future, regardless of which cultural group you belong? What if I told you that *culture is not destiny*?

I am an American. More specifically, I am a Mexican-American. Both my parents came to the United States from Mexico. My cultural background has been very important to me. I honor my Latino cultural legacy. Having grown up in Southern California my entire life, I also am very Americanized. English was not my first language, and it took me many years to learn English effectively. I spent many years in remedial English classes and for many years struggled to keep up with the rest of my classmates in elementary school. I persisted. And persisted. And persisted. I now have a master's degree in Counseling. I was one of the first to finish the thesis requirement from my entire cohort of master's students. I completed one term in a Doctoral program in Clinical Psychology. I also have membership in four nationally and even internationally recognized collegiate interdisciplinary honor societies. I was inducted into Phi Kappa Phi, representing the top five percent of my Alma Mater, California State University, Long Beach. I graduated Cum Laude from CSULB with a 3.8 GPA.

What happened? How did I go from being a struggling student to achieving such phenomenal success? A lot of factors play into this, to be sure. I had very supportive parents. I am an only child; thus a lot of resources could be culled for my success alone. I also put in a fair amount of initiative. What was the source of all this initiative? The dominant culture. I studied that which I

1

saw working well for many mainstream Americans, especially those who were displaying phenomenal results. I then took it upon myself to model those qualities for myself. The results were highly positive. I now want to spread this message to my fellow Latinos so that they can benefit from using this method, which I call *Selective Cultural Adoption* (SCA) as the royal road to success.

Basically, SCA is a means whereby a person becomes like a chameleon in the jungle. The chameleon is able to use its skin to mimic the colors and contours of his surroundings. This enables him to evade predators. It is a highly adaptive method of avoiding danger. The animal blends in. He is indistinguishable from his surroundings. He is successful in that he gets what he needs and goes undetected.

Latino students can become extraordinary students by adopting a chameleon-like method of blending in with certain aspects of American society which will allow Hispanics to move forward. This is not a call to become "whitewashed." Such efforts only ended by pitting Latino against Latino and brother against cultural brother. The assimilationist model of the nineteenth century would be very difficult to put into practice today. However, something must be done to correct the situation that Hispanics currently face. Latinos are now facing a fifty- percent dropout rate from high school. They are dropping out a rate higher than any other ethnic group. This affects not only Hispanics but also all of American society.

We have all seen them: the janitors, the garbage collectors, and the hotel cleaning staff. The cooks in the backs of restaurants. It breaks my heart to see so many Latinos at the bottom of the socioeconomic ladder. It has become a national truth that they are the ones who do the work that no one else wants to do. On the one hand, I suppose it points to a lack of laziness and a willingness to work hard. That is commendable. It also points out that they are not getting into the upper echelons of society. They may do the work that no one else wants to do, but I wish they could rise up in society, refuse to do that work, and allow some other non-Hispanic immigrant group to do the dirty work.

I want to empower Hispanic students to excel. I must stress that my message is not about wholesale adaptation, or forgetting about one's roots. Roots and heritage are very important. They give one a sense of history, and a sense of identity. No one has the right to deny people of any ethnic background their sense of ethnic identity. By the same token, however, it would be naïve to assume that one can immigrate to the United States and feel that one can live as one did in one's native country and still manage to become educated or entrepreneurial. The most disenfranchised Latinos in the United States are the ones who are least assimilated and the ones whose language skills in English are the least developed. They are the ones who insist on living and speaking as if they are still living in their native country. The Latinos who became successful college graduates and became excellent in their chosen field are the ones who made an effort to learn English. I am not referring to basic "street" English. Rather, I am referring to articulate and polished English, with little or no Spanish accent.

In *Foreign Policy Magazine*, April 2004, it was shown that in 1989 to 1990, the education of Mexican-Americans by generation was well behind those of other populations. For instance, of those who were the first generation born here, only 24.7% had a high school diploma. The second generation had a 39.2% graduation rate. The third had a 58.5 % graduation rate, and fourth was 49.4 %. The education of Mexican-Americans and Hispanics in general is well behind those of other groups. I'm particularly concerned about this because of the ramifications that it has not only for Hispanics, but also for American society in general. There is currently a huge underclass in American society comprised of Hispanics, which of course can be broken down into the different Hispanic sub-groups; for instance there are Cubans, Central Americans, South Americans, and of course the largest population, which is Mexicans. According to Samuel Huntington's book *Who Are We?* (2004), in the year 2000, more than 28,000,000 people in the United States spoke Spanish at home, and almost 13.8 million of these spoke English worse than "very well," a 66% increase since 1990. What does this mean overall for Hispanics?

Overall, what these numbers point to is that Hispanics seem to be having difficulty not only graduating from high school but then going on to college and graduating from college. These numbers also mean that they will stay behind as long as they have these educational difficulties.

I was very fortunate that both of my parents believed in education. Yet, what's happening in a lot of Hispanic families and homes is the fact that, while many Hispanics might believe in the principle of the value of education, research has shown that many of them have trouble translating that encouragement into actual concrete steps that they can take to provide a high level of education for their children. According to the Parent Institute for Quality Education, out of every 100 Hispanics who graduates from high school, only two will go on to earn a bachelor's degree. According to the 2003 Almanac Edition of the Chronicle of Higher Education, Hispanics in the United States with a master's degree comprise only 1.9% of the entire Hispanic population. That is a surprisingly small number given the number of Hispanics in the United States. As someone who possesses a master's degree in counseling with a concentration in higher education, I believe that I have a unique perspective that may not have been looked at by other educators in trying to determine why so many Hispanics are failing in their education.

"Scripts," as Eric Berne (1964) referred to them, are playing a large role in causing a lot of Hispanics not to go to college. Scripts are the unspoken, unwritten, implicit messages that many children learn from their families. These messages can be constructive or destructive depending on what is inherent inside the message. Many children receive scripts whose message is positive. This allows them to believe in themselves and go on to pursue very lucrative and successful careers. Other children receive scripts whose message is negative. This causes a child not to believe that he or she is capable of attaining a high level of education or may not be capable or deserving of other things in life. For instance, many young girls receive the messages that they are not worthy or deserving of a healthy, loving relationship with a man. This might be one of several reasons that many women end up in abusive relationships. These messages that parents and cultures send to people can be either very life affirming or very destructive in their effect. My purpose here is to provide a psycho-educational approach to the "nature of the beast" of Hispanic education. Most educators, for instance, want to approach this merely from the point of view of socioeconomic status, pointing to the lower end of the economic and pay scale that Hispanics find themselves at, in order to explain the phenomenon of lower educational achievement. While they may have quite a bit of merit, it certainly does not seem to explain the picture in a complete way.

One case in point is a young Mexican-American woman whom I spoke with recently. She mentioned that her mother had once asked her, "Why would you want to go to college? It's so *boring!*" This young woman was only one semester away from graduation from one of the California State Universities. So, fortunately this message did not reach a level where it programmed her behavior not to go to college, but for a lot of other families, these scripts may have a more de-constructive effect.

As a Mexican-American who was fortunate enough to work my way up to a master's degree level of education, and who has seen the doors that it has opened for me, I have been deeply encouraged to investigate how scripts, socioeconomic status, culture, neighborhoods, peers, all interact to keep Hispanics well behind other groups. I do believe that, as a child grows up, many things need to come together in order for a child to become a high achiever, especially in the home. For instance, a very important factor is the education of the parents. Parents who have gone through the college system in this country know the "ins and outs" of college, what is required to get in, the kind of grades in high school that are necessary to be accepted to a university, and so on. While parents without college degrees might be supportive of the endeavor to send their youngsters off to college, they may not have the requisite knowledge or experience to figure out how to do so. These parents may not be able to give their children the concrete guidance that is necessary to pave the way for a successful college career.

Within the coming decades, this country will be more or less divided culturally and linguistically among Hispanics and non-Hispanic Whites. What will happen if some of these problems related to Hispanic education are not remedied, is that the Hispanic underclass, which are currently the gas-leaf-blowers, hotel cleaning staff, waiters and waitresses, bus boys, and janitors, will continue to grow, and certainly that underclass will never reach the level of prosperity or education that the more dominant Anglo-American group has attained over the years. My purpose in writing this book is to help Hispanics catch up to the other groups in this country: the Anglo-Americans, the Asians, and the Middle Eastern groups, who are all going to the premier colleges and universities in this country, and subsequently attaining cutting-edge jobs.

My position is coming from neither the left nor the right. Those on the left might take a very sympathetic approach to the problem, and feel that the plight of the farm workers and janitors is such that they must save these people, what I call the "Moses Complex." And those on the right feel that if only the U.S. were to reduce illegal immigration from Mexico, and teach English to immigrants, the problem will remedy itself. And I feel that both of those approaches, while they each have merit, are somewhat shortsighted. My position, which is more or less centrist in nature, focuses mainly on what I feel is the logical way out, which is education.

Many things need to come together in order for a student to succeed in school. Success in education does not occur in a vacuum. As with many other ventures, in order to attain a successful outcome, many factors need to be put into place, each in their proper proportion. At times, the factors and their proportions will shift and change depending on the circumstances. However it is clear that many fundamental elements need to be in place in order for a student to matriculate successfully through high school and go on to attain a college degree. Romo and Faldo (1996) found certain measures being taken by Hispanic parents to ensure that their child would graduate from high school. Specifically, they found seven. First, they found that among Hispanics who graduated successfully from high school, the parents were in charge. That is to say, the adolescents never doubted their parents' authority to control and direct their education. Second, they found that authority in the home was not just stemming from the parents to the adolescents. In these homes, the parents not only were the clear authority figures in the homes but also shared a certain amount of influence together with their adolescents. They empowered their adolescents to share and communicate with them their feelings about school and everything that was going on in their lives.

"While the youths acknowledged that their parents were in charge, the parents still listened to the youths and attempted to give them what they wanted when the youths made a good case for it. In this way, the parents trained their children in making decisions for themselves." (p.203).

The third strategy found by these researchers was that these Hispanics set limits. This is related to the first strategy of parents staying in charge. Setting limits allowed for further control to be maintained in the home. The fourth strategy was that parents monitored their student. In this respect, the parents monitored the emotional tone of the adolescent's behavior and monitored the mood and temperament of their youngster in order to keep track of whether there were early signs that something may be wrong and needing remediation. During adolescence, it is important that parents monitor the mood, temperament and indirect communication that teenagers use in order to be able to ascertain the internal world of the adolescent. This will usually be an indicator of whether or not there might be any scholastic problems. The fifth strategy that these parents employed was to keep a tab on the peers that the adolescents would associate with and to draw the line when the peer group seems to be a source of negative influence. It is not surprising that a negative peer group will draw an at risk adolescent away from his or her studies and cause the situation to steadily deteriorate to the point where the at-risk student may finally drop out of school. The sixth strategy that these parents used was that they fed their teenager with the continuous message that they need to stay in school. It is vital that parents continuously replenish the message that education is important. Otherwise, the message begins to be forgotten or downplayed in the mind of the adolescent. Many college graduates to whom I have spoken told me that their parents used to say to them, "When you go to college. . ." or, "After you graduated from college. . ." thus the message became subliminal that college would be an eventuality in the lives of these teenagers once they reached college age. The seventh, and in my belief most important strategy, was that parents were involved with the school and school system of their adolescent. This would take the form of meeting with the instructors or other school officials, and asserting their right to know what was happening in the lives of their adolescents at school. As Romo and Falbo (1996) wrote,

"Youths who graduated knew that their parents were involved in their schooling. These parents scrutinized report cards, talked to teachers and counselors, and even talked to principals, if necessary. The youths knew that their parents had an independent source of information about their school performance, and therefore they knew they could not fool them. The parents who succeeded in keeping their children in school were aggressive in making contacts with their schools. These parents had the social skills to keep the interactions with school staff positive. . ." (p.207)

This brings up a very crucial point for parents and the teachers who interact with them. Parents must make the effort to make teachers their allies and of course, vice versa. When parents approach the school and specifically teachers, with a confrontational or defiant attitude, it will only serve to alienate teachers from parents and ultimately teachers from students. The relationship between teachers and parents is ultimately one of the cornerstones in the matrix of factors affecting the successful completion of an elementary and high school education for youngsters. Teachers also need to be as patient and accommodating with parents as much as is possible. My sympathies lie with teachers who must contend with large and overcrowded classrooms containing upward of 35 students. Nevertheless, like any relationship, it is a two-way interaction requiring effort on both sides as to maintain a harmonious interaction throughout the school year and throughout the entire period of an elementary and high school education. For anyone who works within the educational system of the United States, and interacts with, or serves Latino parents the signs and symptoms of parental underinvolvement must be made known and teachers, educators and staff members of schools must be made aware of these warning signs. As Romo and Falbo (1996) wrote,

> "[The parents of dropouts] did not take charge of their children, they did not engage in two-way influence with their children, they did not set limits on their children's school and social life, they did not closely monitored their children, they did not draw the line between good and bad peers, they did not continuously lectured their children about the value of an education, and they were not involved in their children's school." (p.211)

The nature of the beast is this: Latinos are ranking at or near the bottom of the educational ladder. If nothing is done to alter or improve this situation then all of society will ultimately suffer. Of course, no one will suffer more than Latinos. The problem is rooted in the incompatibility between the culture from which Latinos hail and the culture that is required for educational success in the United States. What must be done in order to correct this is to bring about more attention to this incompatibility and to find out how Latino parents can be made more aware of what is required for educational success in the United States. Until this awareness is brought about in Hispanic parents, Latinos will remain as educationally beleaguered as they currently are. Teachers, counselors, staff members, principals and vice-principals must all work as a single unit within each and every school to invite dialog between themselves and Hispanic parents and help make Hispanic parents aware of how much they as parents need to be involved in the school system. There is currently much debate about the amount of funding for public schools. There is no doubt that adequate funding is required for any school system to operate efficiently and give both students and teachers the resources they need for success. There is also much discussion about safety and gang involvement in certain inner-city schools which has caused many Hispanic students to fear going to school or to fear being attacked on the way to or coming home from school. Safety is necessary, in a very real sense, for any student to feel comfortable enough, and safe enough to go to school. And as much as issues as funding and crime and safety have their merit, what has been omitted, singularly, from the discussion is the impact of culture. Specifically no one wants to discuss how culture has in many ways become a liability for Latinos.

Within the United States we have, at this point in time, a plethora of cultures, and ethnicities. The celebration and emphasis on culture can be traced back to the radicalism of the 1960s. It was at that time that African Americans began to assert their right to form their own cultural power base in groups such as the Black Panthers. At the same time, Latinos began to use the spirit of radicalism of the 1960s to form their own political action groups and committees. This was most evident on the college campuses at the late 1960s. It was at that time that new departments were organized to study Latino culture and Latino history in the United States. They began to form their own university departments and even to coin certain terms, such as *Chicano* or *Brown Power*. As with many radical social movements, the aim was to empower Latinos to "come into their own." This was positive. There have been many injustices that Hispanics, African Americans, Asians and women have had to endure. For over a century, these groups have been looked down upon, demeaned and given unfair working conditions and salaries. Thus, the effort to help minorities and women was quite understandable and noble in its cause. However, the shift that began to occur in these university departments was one in which the efforts to help these groups was becoming less humanitarian, and became more political. Rather that emphasizing cultural unity with all other groups in a spirit of common cause, these university departments began to teach what is in essence, reverse racism. Reverse racism refers mainly to feelings of alienation and antipathy toward anyone who seems to represent the White Anglo-Saxon Protestant (WASP) establishment. There is a beneficial way and a harmful way to bring about social justice and social improvement. These university departments chose the more militant and bellicose way of trying to bring about social justice. The result of this movement was that Hispanics only alienated themselves from mainstream society, without bringing about any real or lasting change in their conditions. Mexican migrant workers still face unbearable working conditions, Hispanics are still at the bottom of the educational ladder, they still are being found in low-wage jobs. Thus, their plight has not improved significantly and they have further retreated themselves from those in the Establishment who could be helping them to enjoy a better life in the United States. Thus, Latinos shot themselves in the foot, and they never were able to attain the improvements they sought for themselves. This is a result of the way in which they were searching for solutions to begin with.

This book is intended for not only for Latino parents but also for teachers, educators, school counselors, school psychologists, principals, and anyone else who serves the Hispanic population within our public and private school system. This book will hopefully show the ways in which Latinos can be helped so that they will truly flourish, enjoying a quality of life within the mainstream of American life. Hispanics can, and should be able to enjoy what is commonly referred to as the American Dream without having to alienate themselves from mainstream society or to become militant and separatists in their cultural orientation. This book will hopefully show how Hispanics can selectively adapt themselves to the educational system of this country, thereby allowing themselves to flourish and go on to graduate from college and enjoy successful careers.

Chapter One

Why I Wrote This Book

As a Mexican-American, I feel a deep sense of concern that comes not really so much out of ethnic loyalty, which I *do* feel toward other Hispanics, but more out of a very basic humanitarian concern I feel for people of *all backgrounds*. I want to help people from every ethnic background—white, black, Hispanic, Asian, and Pacific Islander—who might be at a disadvantage in society. I believe I know the clue to helping ethnic minorities get out of their conundrum. With Hispanics, I see the largest ethnic minority group in American society, and they are coming from many different nations. The preponderance, of course, of the Hispanic immigrants are coming from Mexico. Understandably, the ones who migrate are, by and large, those from the less advantaged classes. Therefore, they are going to have more difficulty fitting into American society, assimilating, and learning the language. As President John F. Kennedy reminded us, we all got off the boat at one point, and that's very true. Certain other groups have had the good fortune to be able to jump into American society and "hit the ground running," so to speak, by learning the language and learning the ropes of the educational system. Hispanics hail from predominantly agricultural areas in Latin America and later settled in large urban areas, such as the county of Los Angeles. They come from a very different culture with a different set of expectations and different values. If we contrast this with the Irish migration in the mid-nineteenth century, we find a similar agrarian background. However, the Irish already spoke English, even if it was with an accent, and this allowed them to adapt themselves to the American scene. With Hispanics, the process has become a little bit more complex. First of all, as has been pointed out, there is a close proximity between the United States and Mexico. This causes large numbers of immigrants to come into the United States and it seems that their ancestral home is just a couple of hundred miles away. What happens is that the proximity of the United States and Mexico causes many Hispanics to feel that they don't really have to assimilate. Nor do they feel that they should have to learn the English language. There are large ethnic communities in California, and indeed all over the country, where large numbers of Hispanics speak Spanish, and therefore they don't feel the need to learn English, or to learn American culture. This presents some challenges. First of all, when they send their children to school, the school may or may not be equipped with bilingual teachers.

I grew up in Lakewood, California, and attended a parochial Catholic school, and most of my teachers were Irish nuns. When I went to school, I, like many other Hispanics, knew mostly Spanish and very little English. By the time I was in the second grade, my second grade teacher had a conference with my mother, who told her, "You either teach this boy English or go back to Mexico." I had the good fortune of having two very bright and intelligent parents who, immediately that afternoon, turned 180 degrees and began to speak to me only in English. All the television programs, all the books, all the movies, everything from then on were strictly in English. And even then, the damage was not corrected right away. It took several years of being in remedial English classes and catching up that finally allowed me to reach parity with my other classmates. Twenty-five years later, and with passage of Proposition 227 in California, many Hispanics are now faced with the challenge of having to learn English. Samuel Huntington's data, as reported in *Foreign Policy Magazine* in 1990, showed that about 95% of Mexican-born immigrants spoke Spanish at home, 73.6% of these did not speak English very well, and 43% of Mexican born individuals were "linguistically isolated." He goes on to write that in 1999, some 753,505 presumably second-generation students in Southern California schools who spoke Spanish at home were not proficient in English. Latinos in the United States must learn English, and not expect American institutions to accommodate them by having bilingual staff and bilingual personnel.

This is a direct reversal of the pattern of assimilation of earlier centuries in the United States. A century ago, America's major institutions would more or less first welcome immigrants with open arms but then would quite understandably hope that they would learn the language and adapt themselves to the national culture. Like any relationship, it's a two-way street. Any healthy relationship requires "give and take" on both sides, and requires accommodation on both sides. The current pattern that we are witnessing with regard to Latino immigration to the United States seems to be somewhat lopsided. Latinos want the United States to recognize their traditions, their culture, their music, and their food, and especially their language, but they themselves seem to be making little effort to learn the language of the United States and learn American customs, American cultural history, and American institutions. This phenomenon would probably not be of any real concern at all if it weren't for the fact that Hispanics right now are lagging behind other ethnic groups in education and socioeconomic status.

Julian E. Barns, a writer for *U.S. News & World Report*, March 22 to March 29, 2004, citing information from the National Center for Educational Statistics, reported that the total percentage of Latino students who graduated from high school was 57% in the year 2000. In the same year, 79% of African-Americans graduated from high school, and 89% of Anglo-Americans graduated. This article went on to say, "In high schools, the situation is . . . dismaying. Black and Hispanic seniors on average read and do math only as well as white eighth-graders." So the assimilation and education, socioeconomic status, and culture of Latinos are all inextricably mixed together.

My message is twofold. First, I wish to untangle each of these elements to see what factors contribute to the problems. Secondly, I seek to propose solutions to those problems so that future generations of young Latino children are not caught in the same quagmire as the current high school population. I want to make sure that each Latino child who is raised in the United States has the same chance to go to college as I did. The message needs to be conveyed to Latinos in general, and Latino parents in particular, that if they really try and persevere, they can make something of themselves and become ambitious, intelligent, contributing members of society.

By becoming intelligent and contributing members of American society, Latinos can make more informed choices, including choices that directly affect the quality of their own lives. There is no limit to the areas in which Latinos can then go on to make better choices for themselves and for their families, including health, finances, career moves, occupational decisions, and even choices that are on a grander scale such as whom to vote for president in any national election. Within the Latino culture itself, there is also another area where Latinos must become more critical thinkers and critical consumers of information; there are a host of scam artists and other charlatans who are all too willing to make money off of the uninformed masses who may not understand they are being conned out of their money. So another benefit of becoming more educated is that an individual is able to spot a scam artist or anyone else who might be preying on uneducated individuals hoping to take their money.

When I reference Latin culture, I have many countries in mind. I broadly refer to the countries between the northern tip of Mexico, all the way down to Tierra Del Fuego, Argentina. Certainly, each country is going to have its own unique history, wars, triumphs, victories, independence holidays, national cuisine, and folkloric dress. All of those things, and many more, go to make up the culture of a country, and each of those elements is very vital to that culture. The culture of any country will be shaped by the way people interact with each other and by the manner in which that collective of citizens interacts with other nations. It is unfair, at times, to group together peoples from many different nations who share broad characteristics. Such groupings ignore the unique character, distinctiveness, history and culture of each of those different nations that, together, make up an ethnic region. For instance, when one speaks or writes of Asian culture in general terms, one overlooks the fact that Asian culture is comprised of many countries. Each of those different countries has a unique culture. To make a point one must at times speak or write in general terms. Even within each nation, there are normally variations in the individual cultures of the families in that nation. Furthermore, there are always going to be unique psychological differences from one person to the next, even within an extended or nuclear family unit.

The experience that one national group will have emigrating to another country will be shaped by the way in which the two cultures interact. In the early 1600s, the English Separatists, which can broadly be referred to as Puritans, left London and the universities of Oxford and Cambridge and founded a colony in Leyden, Holland. There they attempted to rear their English children in a manner that was consistent with and parallel to the culture they had known in England. They ran into obstacles, however, as succeeding generations of English children were being raised as Dutch children and learning the Dutch language and beginning to forget their English heritage. The children were beginning to adopt Dutch ways of dressing and their parents felt concerned that their children were not being raised within the English culture. Within a few generations, the elders of the English Puritan community were dying destitute in their old age as a result of not being able to find adequate employment due to the language barrier. Those of the younger generation who were adopting the Dutch language and culture, in order to survive, were losing much of what had gone to make English Puritanism unique. This was beginning to become a grim lifestyle for the English settlers. They were strangers in a strange land. Their feelings were understandable. The language was different, the folk dress was different, the music was different; indeed everything was different. It was *not English*. After a few generations, it became apparent that the English settlement in Holland could not continue. The Puritans left Holland and established what was to become the Massachusetts Bay Colony. They chose not to adapt themselves to the Dutch culture. This caused their venture in Holland to fail.

Many other groups coming to America have faced a similar situation. In the mid-nineteenth century, the Irish escaping the Irish Potato Plague left the Emerald Isle and settled on the Eastern shores of the United States, in cities such as Boston. They later migrated farther inland to the upper Midwest, into such cities as Chicago. The Irish also brought with them their own unique cultural heritage that was Celtic in origin and beautiful in its own right. Later generations of Germans, Swedes, and Norwegians began to follow the same patterns of migration. In the early twentieth century, thousands of Armenians fled the genocide at the hands of the Turks, and settled in large numbers in California. In the late 1930s, many Jewish immigrants, anxious to escape Nazi oppression, settled into the United States. In the mid-1970s, after the fall of Saigon to the Communists, many Cambodian "Boat People" fled Southeast Asia and settled into various cities in the United States. The images that Americans have seen on their television sets are those of old frigates loaded with starving Chinese immigrants who were desperate to reach the shores of San Francisco. They had faced privations, hunger and even emaciation in making the long ocean journey for the mere chance at a better life in the United States. Lastly, the largest and most recent group of immigrants into the United States has been from Latin America in general, and Mexico in particular. The images, stories and haunting visages of all these groups evokes in the most callous of television viewers pity and even a touch of admiration of the bravery of such people to risk life and limb to arrive in America.

What has given these groups, and many others, their strength, is the fact that they are a group of individuals stemming from a single ethnic and cultural background. This strength gives the group a sense of unity; livelihood; and a common cause. History will show that group membership will be strengthened when there is a shared cause. This can be readily observed in any nation when there is a natural catastrophe, such as a powerful earthquake. This is also evident when there is a man-made event with devastating consequences, such as a war. So certainly, having a common purpose, a common background, a common past, and common goals for the future, is what can give the people of any background a sense of internal and external strength. On a very local level, one can observe this unifying energy in intercollegiate sporting events involving two colleges. On a national level, one can observe it in the pride of watching one's national team in the Olympics.

What happened in Holland with the Puritan settlers is a classic example where one culture was incompatible with another. Although their religious backgrounds may have been similar, the English settlers were not able to adapt themselves to the Dutch cultural landscape. They chose not to acculturate or assimilate themselves to Holland. However, they felt it was in their best interest to migrate to a land where they would not have to share space, and thus compromise culturally, and compete vocationally, with anyone else. They left their temporary settlement in Leyden and settled along the northeastern coast of the American continent.

Given the fact that the amount of uninhabited space in the world has decreased and we are more and more forced to share land with other people and to coexist elbow to elbow with others, then there are now some fundamental questions which we must ask ourselves. For instance, if we are to co-exist, in one stretch of land, such as the Continental United States, then the question becomes: How can we make cultures compatible and how can we find the elements of one culture which can be readily accepted by the other in a process of mutual give-and-take? Two cultures that live side by side stand to learn and gain much from each other; and gain each other's trust and respect. They can become a source of mutual strength, unity and assistance in times of crises. If two cultures can become a source of strength, unity and assistance, then certainly in a country such as ours that has many different ethnicities, cultures and backgrounds, this strength unity and assistance can be multiplied by a large exponent, thereby enrich, unify and strengthen the American landscape.

I am convinced that the United States has benefited from this large influx of individuals and groups of people from other countries. These immigrants have brought with them the richness of their cultural heritage and the spiritual vitality of their homeland. I feel that the United States has and will continue to benefit from this influx of individuals who bring with them the education, background, training, vocational skills and innovation, which have gone to make this country so strong.

My former thesis advisor at the University of La Verne, where I earned my master's degree, once told me of the reason that the faculty at La Verne had been chosen from a diverse background. The professors had been carefully selected from diverse ethnic backgrounds because each person brings with him or her unique perspectives of the material that may not have been possible had the entire faculty been of a homogeneous background. Having this plurality of ethnicities helped to bring new perspectives on concepts as diverse as Sigmund Freud's drive theory or methods of pedagogy. The colleges of this country need faculties that bring with them a diverse set of values and a diverse set of perspectives.

In the coming decades, I do believe that America should welcome those who bring with them talents and strengths and intelligence that may not yet exist in this country, and whose import will be a source of future strength for America. In the end, I am very much in favor of the immigration of individuals possessing skills that are needed, and are in high demand by our free market economy and our technological infrastructure, and our avant-garde universities. America has been without a doubt strengthened by the skills, the perceptions, the strength, the beauty, the integrity of so many people that have come here from so many backgrounds. No other nation in the world has enjoyed such a rich and diverse background as has the

United States. The *noble experiment* succeeded. This success is owed to
our national diversity.

This work is not the first to investigate how culture can have an impact
upon educational success in the United States. The late Professor John Ogbu,
Ph.D., who was an educational anthropologist focused precisely on this area.
Dr. Ogbu found that there are two minority groups. First, there are the voluntary immigrants. There are groups, such as Asians, who come to the United
States in the hopes of building a better life. The voluntary immigrants have
positive expectations and a positive outlook on life in the United States and
rear their children in a way that inculcates a reverence for the institutions, values, and resources of the United States. Involuntary immigrant groups, such
as African Americans, and in our present study, Latinos, are those who out of
historical precedent ended up in the United States under less than ideal circumstances. These less than ideal circumstances would be, for instance,
linked to slavery for African Americans and redistribution of land for Mexicans in the United States. The patterns that Dr. Ogbu soon began to discover
was that among voluntary immigrants there is a positive expectation about
life in the United States, and for the children of these immigrants, positive expectations for school. Among the involuntary immigrant groups, there is a
less favorable and more defiant and oppositional stance against the dominant
culture and its institutions such as schools.

He defined primary cultural differences to be those things such as language, music, or religion that can become the salient differences between two
populations. An example would be an East Indian Hindu family living next
door to a Midwestern Lutheran family. Each family will have a different religion, language, music, forms of dress, and traditions. He defined secondary
cultural differences as the differences that are evident after any kind of interaction between the two cultural groups has already taken place. Thus, he sees
the defiant or oppositional culture of involuntary immigrant groups as a result
of the interaction between the involuntary population and the dominant white,
Anglo-Saxon culture of the United States. Other researchers (Ibanez, Kuperminc, Jurkovic, Perilla, 2004, p.560), have used other, similar terms to describe the work of Dr. Ogbu, such as *cultural attributes* to refer to those characteristics which separate two cultures before contact occurs, akin to Dr.
Obgu's *primary cultural differences* and *cultural adaptations* which are similar to the term *secondary cultural differences* as explained by Dr. Ogbu.
Thus, it is my sincerest hope that this book will contribute to the work began
by Dr, Ogbu in his research at the University of California when he was investigating African American educational challenges. Ibanez, Kuperminc, Jurkovic, and Perilla (2004) found that,

"There seem to be both cultural attributes and cultural adaptations involved in how Latino youth perceive school experiences and achievement motivation. In terms of cultural attributes, schooling belonging appears to relate to achievement motivation for all Latino youth, regardless of generation or language acculturation level." (p. 567)

Thus it is both gratifying and reassuring to see that others have begun the process of investigating these cultural phenomenons and hopefully this book will be able to shed light on the reasons that Hispanics have had such trouble attaining parity with other cultural groups within the United States.

Chapter Two

Latin American Culture

Latin American culture can loosely be said to have several characteristics. First, there is an undeniable strength of family ties. There are strong ties between the generations, and it is not unusual to find several generations living under one roof. As the movement from Latin America spreads upward into the United States, the original flavor, the original character and stamp of the original culture may be somewhat diluted in the eventual inter-generational process of immigrating into the United States. What may be the norm in Miami, or in New York City, or in Los Angeles Hispanic populations may not necessarily be what might be found in their native Cuba, Puerto Rico or Mexico, respectively.

Economics play a factor in how the culture changes through the different socio-economic strata. The culture of a wealthy Mexican family living on the outskirts of Mexico City in their private hacienda with marble tile floors and several maids will be very different from the culture of an impoverished Mexican family living in one of the many poor suburbs of Los Angeles, which are normally gang infested areas. One has to look at the way culture changes and morphs, depending on the location and the socio-economic condition of the area in which the family lives. Certainly, in times of trouble or distress, it is only natural that people will band together for protection in a group. What one may see as a very tightly held community within the Latin American ethnic neighborhoods, may very well be the result of the duress that they experience as part of the culture shock of coming to this country. They purposely seek communities where they will find others who are like themselves, and "hide" in those enclaves so as to buffer themselves from the shock of life in the United States. There is strength in numbers, as the old saying goes, and Latinos use this age-old truth when they congregate in their *barrios*.

The culture that one finds among Latino communities in the United States will have as their characteristics a focus on the family, several generations living within one house, and a tendency to marry at a younger age than one would find in the dominant Caucasian group. Another characteristic of Latino culture is the tendency to have many children within the family. On a cultural level, it is axiomatic that a young Hispanic couple will have many children during their years of marriage. This would not present a problem to Latinos were it not for the fact that it is usually the poorest Latino families that have many children. This only makes their economic problems even worse. Furthermore, it diminishes the amount of time and attention that can be given to any single child's education. It is a well-known fact that first and only children are able to achieve the highest levels of education and achievement. There are those who claim that the size of Hispanic families is caused by avoidance of birth control measures due to religious sanctions by the Catholic Church. However, this notion is rather misguided. If one observes Roman Catholic families in Germany, Italy, France, and certain other Northern European countries one finds Catholic piety, and at the same time, enough collective wisdom among those families to keep their family size small. Thus the argument that the Catholic Church is to blame for large Hispanic families doesn't hold much weight when compared to European Catholic families that are small in size. Rather than attacking the Catholic Church, one must again look at the culture and realize that the Latino culture itself is to blame for the emphasis on large families.

In many poor and underdeveloped countries, now turned less developed countries (LDCs), especially those whose economies depend on agriculture, the tendency to marry young and have large families has an adaptive survival value. In Africa, for instance, the farmer who has many children, especially sons, will be ensured that the next generation can till and harvest the land. In many poor countries it is vital that a man have many children in order to have labor available to him, and to have successors to his agricultural business. Thus, the tendency to have large families with many children can have either a positive or negative effect, depending on the circumstances. For Latinos living within the United States, this will have a negative effect due to the fact that these families are living in cities. There is no opportunity for them to use their children as farm hands or as progenitors who will inherit a large agricultural enterprise from which to make money. Thus, having large families works against Hispanics living in the United States.

Generally there is a strong emphasis on independence in the Latin American culture that is slightly different from the dominant Anglo-Saxon culture that I will be describing later. The independence that one sees in the Latin American young, and specially in the males, stems from a widely held cultural belief that when one reaches a certain age around 18, one must then display to himself and to the world his ability to be a full grown man. In this case, that becomes manifested by the early attainment of almost any source of employment that seems viable and stable. The cultural emphasis is on finding employment, and maintaining that employment at all costs.

I learned recently from a woman from Mexico City that in her native country, if one is smart enough, fast enough, and possesses enough savvy, one can under the right circumstances, and with a little luck, begin to market a product or sell some kind of service and actually stand to produce an income that might be comparable to some of the other professionals who might already possess degrees from one of the Mexican universities.

In Mexico, there is a kind of free-for-all market economy where, on one end of the spectrum, lie the extreme rich, and on the other end, the poor and destitute. Among the less advantaged members of Mexican society, there is a perception that if one has something unique to peddle in the streets, or in the marketplace, one can get very lucky and make money. These people feel that they could, if they are savvy enough and clever enough, gain access to some of the material privileges comparable to that of someone who graduated from a university. For many entrepreneurs in Mexico, this has been the case. When Latin American immigrants come to the United States, two cultural realizations should take place within their minds. First, they should honor their roots. They should honor their country of origin. The United States as mentioned previously, has benefited greatly from the rich cultural influx of emigration. Migration has made the United States the superpower that it is. Thus immigrants should take every necessary measure in order to honor, remember, and even visit their country of origin. This would no doubt be a source of pride and warm feelings for the emigrant. The second step that must occur within the minds of the immigrants is that they must look at cultural patterns within the United States that will be to their advantage to emulate. Life in the United States is usually very different from the way of life that the emigrant knew in his or her native country. Most evident in the United States is a different philosophy about achievement, time and money, ambition, rugged individualism, material comforts, and the role of government. For our purposes here, let us focus on education. In Latin America, it can be a sign of success merely to have graduated from the twelfth grade. Many immigrants to the United States from Latin America may not have even had the chance or opportunity to even reach twelfth grade. They may have only reached the tenth or even the eighth grade. Thus when they arrive in the United States, what they may or may not realize is that in this country, there is a stronger need to go to a college or university. Why is this so? The most obvious reason is that the ever-increasing population in the United States forces the market economy that we have, to demand a more educated work force. Perhaps if the population of the United States were still small, there would not be as great a need within the marketplace to hire educated workers. However, with the population size that we have now, there is a need among employers in general to hire the brightest employees they can find. In addition, there has always been a strong emphasis on education in the United States. The Founding Fathers were strong advocates for literacy and education and it became engrained within the cultural fabric of the United States to emphasize a college education.

The other cultural trait that is very much at heart of Latin American culture, has to do with the love of music, a love of dancing, a love of parties, and stage-of-life festivities such as "quinceaneras", and fiestas which are normally very festive.

Within the culture of Latin America the male has been characterized by the "machismo" phenomenon. This mindset values masculinity in a manner that is somewhat different than the way it is valued in the United States. It emphasizes exaggerated displays of strength, virility, and power. This is manifested in the muscle cars, with modified engines, to give the car its extra power. It can then be followed up with expensive chrome wheels. There is also a need to display physical strength in the body by working up the biceps, or having a bulky frame. Tattoos are common. Large and weighty gold chains or medallions, many with the Virgin Mary, are common. The ability to consume large amounts of beer is valued. This is usually in league with the consumption of the more "manly" drinks, such as Tequila. Even male sexuality is expressed through the conquest of a woman. There is no surrender, or vulnerability in his sexual experience, merely an emphasis on how long the man can sustain the union, or how many times he can bring the woman to orgasm.

The Latin American male, or at least the United States variety, has a strong need to display his independence. He needs to display to the world his autonomy, or at least in the eyes of his peers, and to his "woman". This usually begins to manifest itself when the male turns eighteen. At that moment, he is seen as a full "man." Now that he is eighteen, he can work, earn a paycheck, and enlist in the Army, or any branch of the Armed Forces. He can vote. He can move out of his parents' home. There is a keen eagerness to enter the working world. This is admirable. It is certainly not a sign of slothfulness. No one can be lazy and yet at the same time so eager to enter the working world and earn a living. The problem becomes one of not realizing the higher earnings capability they would have if in the possession of a college degree. They could be earning even more if they were to possess a Master's degree. What is truly paradoxical is the fact that these males feel that they can do anything at age eighteen, yet college is not one of the things they feel they can take on. This description overlooks the high numbers of Hispanic males who are graduating from college in the United States, as well as in Latin America. Yet, in terms of sheer representation in the United States, the proportion of Hispanics in college, or, more to the point, graduating with a four-year degree, is truly low.

How can we better explain this phenomenon? First, if there is no one in the family who has gone to college, it will seem a somewhat overwhelming task to figure out how to go to college. One usually needs a role model, someone in the family who has traversed the college terrain before and can serve as a navigator. So, lack of someone in the immediate family is certainly one factor. Another factor is the misperception that college is too expensive. Another factor is that youngsters, as well as their parents, may not be informed about the college preparatory classes that need to be taken immediately upon enrollment in high school. Yet another factor which may explain the reluctance on the part of many Latin men in the United States is the cultural ethos of maintaining strong emotional and geographic ties to one's family of origin, usually one's nuclear unit. This discourages many Latino high school graduates from going to college, especially if it is located far away.

For many Latin males and females, the idea or concept of being geographically distant from their families is difficult to bear. I can relate to this as I missed my father very much when I was training to become a Peace Corps volunteer in Eastern Europe in what appeared to be the edge of the world. There evolves the strong wish to be close to their parents, especially when they begin to see their parents showing the infirmity of old age. They feel it is their duty to be nearby as a source of help. There is absolutely nothing wrong with this. As a matter of fact, it is somewhat comforting in this age of displacement and transient lifestyles that at least some pockets of our population are making the effort to stay in one geographic area long enough to be useful to those who will, in the end, be very much in need of assistance. There may be times when a young Latin American student will be given the chance to attend a university in another state, even on the other side of the country. *The ties to the family, in part, will mitigate whether he or she chooses to take that offer or not.*

The Latin American woman shares some characteristics of the Latin American male, but there are also some distinct differences. In many Hispanic homes, when there is more than one daughter, it falls on the oldest daughter to stay and live at home until marriage. The aim is to keep her at home and have her assist the parents in raising her younger siblings, and of course to play the role of Florence Nightingale to the infirm parents once they are older. The oldest daughter is not to leave the home, lest the family chastise her. The thought of living on her own, or living with another female roommate in a college dorm, is simply not entertained. At this point, one might be tempted to ask: What about all the Latina college students dorming at UCLA, or other eastern universities in the United States? One could argue: Surely, some of those Hispanic women must be oldest daughters! That argument undoubtedly is correct. However, those Hispanic women in question (and the Hispanic men in the men's dorms) are clearly not going along with the traditional arrangement of gender rules and cultural sanctions which prohibit a lot of young Latin American women from going to college.

In addition, among Latino cultural values, there is a strong bias in favor of large families. Motherhood is the option of choice for many women. Is it a choice? Or is it tradition? Many Latin American women feel that it is their duty to "give" their husbands a child, especially a son. This is reminiscent of the favoritism shown to baby boys in China. The female is seen by the male as the baby maker, the lover-on-demand, the cook, the nanny, maid, and teacher for the children, if they are lucky to receive any pedagogy from her at all. It is felt that her place is "home and hearth". While the male is to show off his virility, the female is seen as embodying fertility. The quinceanera is the large and lively celebration of a fifteen-year old girl's transition to young womanhood. Many relatives will come to her parents' house to join in the festivities. The girl normally wears a large white dress, not too dissimilar to the one she will be wearing a few years down the road when she gets married. In very rural and in poor families, much festiveness and food, drinking and music mark occasions such as these. The girl has come of age. In other parts of the world, such as in Africa, one can readily see these stage-of-life ceremonies taking place. Adolescent girls in Africa are given their own version of the quinceanera. The older women of the tribe will sing and dance along with the young women, who have usually experienced menarche, and are now formally welcomed into the tribal village as full women. From a cultural anthropological perspective, these ceremonies serve a very important function. They serve to give everyone in the tribe, or group, a very unique sense of belonging, and place, and a sense of being an important part of the group. They serve to make the tribe feel that they have withstood centuries, even millennia of hardship, intact and with their culture totally preserved. This is vital to the perpetuity of any cultural group. One can see the importance of Bar Mitzvahs for Jewish adolescent boys and their families. After all the pogroms and religious and sociopolitical prosecution that they have endured, it is important for the Jews to feel that they can preserve that which has made their culture special and unique without outside interference. That is why many Jewish parents still take many of their children to Hebrew-language schools and have their children taught by rabbis.

With regard to the above descriptions of the cultural world of the Latina, there is a darker side to its rules and proscriptions. For instance, all the pomp and celebration which is given to the quinceanera more or less "locks in" the future choices for the young girl. How is this so? The more the traditional culture venerates the standardized role of the Latina, the more it will coax her into choices, which, in the United States, may serve ultimately to keep her at a socioeconomic level below that of Anglo-American women. In the United States, as opposed to other countries, it is normally those with advanced college degrees who are able to get the one-way ticket out of poverty. They are able to enjoy independence, careers with higher earning potential, enjoy greater marketability, attain social status, and enjoy certain fruits, such as the house with the white picket fence and the luxury sports utility vehicle, the ubiquitous SUV. Another cultural distinction between the United States and other countries is that in this country, women are encouraged to follow their own dream, husband or no husband, boyfriend or no boyfriend. However, in the traditional Latin American culture, the woman is to depend on the husband to provide all these things. She is to get these things, if lucky, through his efforts. The current poverty level for Hispanics in the United States points to the fact that *the males are not providing enough for their families through their own efforts.* Thus, if Latinas are to gain an equal footing with Anglo-American and Asian-American women, then they must reconsider their cultural legacy with regard to women's roles in the family. This is not to say that Latinas cannot be close to their families or loved ones. Indeed, family togetherness can be a source of great comfort and love for many people. It is a source of rich emotional nourishment. However, Latinas must look at their own goals and dreams, and they must decide if those goals and dreams will be accomplished by choosing the traditional familial path dictated by the culture. In the end, a woman's self-esteem will be stronger knowing that whatever success came her way was the result of her own initiative and her own efforts.

The role of the extended family cannot be overemphasized in the Latino culture. It is not uncommon to find aunts, uncles, cousins, and especially grandparents living in a Hispanic household. This can have both positive as well as negative results. On the positive side, having the extended family living under one roof keeps loneliness at bay. It allows intergenerational contact for young children, which allows the youngsters to absorb some of their grandparents' wisdom, through osmosis. This can also lift the burden off the parents of constantly chasing after and looking after the children if the grandparents can play the role of babysitter. The parents can have their own "hot date" night out while the grandparents watch the children. They can, of course, trust the in-laws of either spouse to safely handle the children while they go out to rekindle the romance of their marriage. There is a downturn to all this. If the household contains relatives from the extended family or grandparents living within its walls, then the home will most likely have a chaotic environment within it. Children need a safe, quiet home where they can study. Their home may be safe, but is it quiet? Are there cousins running around the house? Is the television always turned on? Are there children in front of the television set playing video games? If there is a computer in the home, is it being used only to download music from the Internet? Or to play games online? Are the parents constantly talking back and forth with the grandparents from one room to another? The mind is like a mirror; it reflects back what is in front of it. If a child comes from a home with chaos, the child's mind will reflect that chaos. In order for the child to have the tranquility of mind, sustained attention span and tenacity, the main ingredients for academic success, the child's home must encourage this. Children need a safe quiet place where they can study. This can be the dining table, converted to that usage before or after dinner.

With all the commotion that can occur within the home where several relatives reside, it also becomes more difficult for students to have direct feedback from their parents regarding homework. Although the responsibility rightly falls on the student to complete his or her homework on time, the student benefits greatly when parents become involved. The child needs to feel that his or her parents care and are as involved as possible in the education he or she is receiving. This involves asking the child what sort of day he or she had at school, what material is being covered in class, what kind of homework needs to be completed, and the due dates of the assignments. The child will also benefit greatly from parental involvement at the school. This entails more than the customary Parent-Teacher conferences held twice each year. School festivities, fund-raising drives, and field trips are all integral to school life, and the more that parents can directly participate in such activities, the less isolated the child will feel in plowing through the academic material and social uncertainties of school life.

The teachers of the school systems cannot be expected to provide, in its entirety, the self-discipline, structure, guidance, and quietude that the child should be receiving from home. Instead of the parents providing all of these, there is a tendency in the Latino culture to live for the moment, which is characteristic of many cultures on this planet that have had to endure centuries and centuries of hardship and colonization and privation. The national ethos then begins to become one of wanting to at least live for today because one never knows what might happen tomorrow. One must enjoy whatever small comforts one can, in a single day, because tomorrow God, the forces of nature, the government, the dictator, guerrilla groups or some kind of oppressive regime may take it away.

In many cultures, one finds a present-centered life style focused on finding, for instance, immediate employment, or immediate enjoyment of a fiesta.

It is usually within the more industrialized nations that one finds more planning and forward thinking in the populace. This stands to reason, in a sense, because as a nation becomes stronger economically and politically, and even militarily, one can afford to think about the future because one assumes one will be there in the future, both on an individual and on a national basis. Ironically, there has been a trend in modern psychology, what one might term "pop psychology," to publish books that teach modern corporate Americans to enjoy more out of each day, and not to be so driven to work. There is now a very real and viable movement to emphasize to them the comforts of family and loved ones, spirituality and time for oneself, so as to get more enjoyment and satisfaction out of each day. This of course happens within the context of a future thinking and forward moving society.

With regard to education, what is necessary to inculcate into the Latino communities of the United States, is the perception that it is good to plan for the future; it is good to invest time, energy and effort into the future. The Hispanic culture has transplanted into the United States the "living for the moment" mindset that is so common in Latin America as a result of poverty.

For many Latin Americans the disparity between the cultural values of the country from which they hail, and the new cultural values from the United States can be quite discernible. What must occur is that Latin Americans must begin to abandon the values they may have had about success in education, in their native country, and adapt a new set of values based upon educational success within the United States. Thus, if an emigrant comes to the United States with a tenth grade education he or she will have to see to it that their child or children will exceed that level of education and go on to become college graduates.

The clue as to why Hispanics do not invest as much as they should in education may stem from the notion of time within the Hispanic culture. Within the Latin American culture there is an emphasis on living only for the present moment. There is less emphasis on investing in the future. This contrasts with other cultures that are more future-oriented.

Investing in the future is an Anglo-Saxon cultural value, while living for the moment is a Latin American value. With regard to education, if Latin Americans are to advance themselves, they must begin to use their notion of time somewhat differently from what they have been used to. There is the old saying that Hispanics live in the land of *manana*. Well, that may or may not be true, but certainly the American culture has a strong emphasis on time and expediency. It is important to teach the Latin Americans of the United States that what they do today will have an impact on their future. In other words, they have to be constantly vigilant that today has an impact on tomorrow, that the investments they make today will become manifest tomorrow. And that is where the importance of education lies: in its future benefits and rewards.

We are truly faced with a clash of cultures. This time it is not an East meets West cultural clash but a "South meets North." And in this south meets north clash, the ultimate aim is for every immigrant group to feel good about what they have brought to the American landscape, to retain everything they can, but at the same time to adapt themselves to certain adoptable traits that they see in the American landscape. This is very similar to what has been called by social researchers Social Darwinism.

Social Darwinism uses the principles laid out by Charles Darwin and other naturalist who expanded the theory that certain animal species developed traits and changes in their structure in order to better adapt themselves to nature and to survive by escaping predators and being able to propagate their own species. Decades later, that same paradigm was used to justify inequities between whites and blacks. The theory was that blacks in the United States did not have the traits that were adaptive to their survival. That was supposed to explain why blacks were behind everyone else and needing advancement. This movement has been manipulated by unscrupulous social scientists in order to justify their own racist beliefs.

Yet one can use Social Darwinism either constructively or destructively depending on the paradigm on which it is operating. With regard to Latin American acculturation and assimilation into the United States, the hope is that Latinos learn the value of education. We might be able to adapt Social Darwinism more ethically to say that Latin Americans will be better able to thrive and flourish in the United States if and when they adapt the cultural traits of educated Anglo Americans who become successful in life.

Charles Darwin observed that no animal changes its shape in any drastic way in order to adapt and thrive; rather, animals merely changed in subtle ways so as to blend with their environment. We can use this metaphor to claim that Latin Americans should in no way make drastic changes in their cultural composition. Latinos should in no way diminish the many wonderful qualities that make them Latin Americans. This is not a call for Latin Americans to divest themselves of who they are. *Latin Americans should be proud to be Latin Americans.* Along with that pride, however, should come a concomitant effort to adapt the work ethic, study ethic, learning ethic, critical thinking ethic that is part of the dominant culture of the United States: the Anglo Protestant culture.

What has made the cultural experience of Latinos in the United States as problematic as it is, is their tendency to feel, experience, and vocalize an ambiguity about their homeland. Many Hispanics come to the United States in search of a better life yet curiously, after a duration of time in the United States, nostalgia begins to set in and they will see any criticism of their home country as blasphemy. There is a contradiction in their position. They do not realize that their contradiction is quite obvious. If they thought their home country was as wonderful and splendid as they remember it to be, or is professed to be, then why do they come to the United States? Surely, if they were willing to leave everything behind, then they certainly saw more incentive in coming to the United States than in staying in their native country. Why is this so? The answer seems to lie in the fact that the Latino emigrant will come to the United States without becoming properly assimilated. This lack of assimilation will ultimately cause the Latinos to remain poor, living within an ethnically isolated *barrio*, and not having the material comforts or the occupational success they had hoped for when they originally arrived. It is at that point that the failure is perceived that the nostalgia begins. It is quite clear that some sort of failure within the United States precipitates the nostalgia. They remain poor, or their children are now adolescent mothers or their boys are in gangs, or they have been living within a crime-ridden ghetto from which they cannot escape. Their minds then begin to travel back to that place from which they came in an effort to sooth themselves with sugar coated imagery which is most likely not based in fact. There is a very basic tendency within the human mind to escape in fantasy to a time and place when life was perceived to have been simpler, happier, and nicer. Some social scientists have noted this phenomenon. Victor Davis Hanson (2003) wrote: "For the Mexican immigrant. . . . A limited visitation, a family reunion-but usually not a permanent return-nourished enough nostalgia for Mexico to war with the creation of a truly American identity." (p. 22) Yet, as he correctly points out, "The reality is that, despite the grandiose boasts, the protestations of undying allegiance and the menacing outbursts of national pride, few immigrants ever really want to return to Mexico. Very few wish to live as they did in Mexico . . . none wish to replenish their roots by moving their families to rural Mexico and a world of untreated sewage, parasite-infested water and herbalists standing for cardiologists." (p. 23)

Thus, the Latino emigrant and especially for the Mexican emigrant, this double-standard, what one might even term a type of *cultural hypocrisy*, is that many Hispanics come to the United States criticizing the country from which they came, but then ultimately criticize their host country, the United States, in which they now live, and romanticizing the recollections of their mother country. As Hanson (2003) points out,

> "It is common to hear those millions who come here slander Mexico to their new neighbors-which is logical, given their brutal treatment and low expectations back there; but just as frequently, nostalgia and romance gradually take over and make Mexico more attractive as it grows more distant . . . this newly romanticized Mexico of primal force and natural virtue has made strong claims on the heart of the new arrival, and thus has been ever more deleterious to his odyssey of becoming an American." (p. 33)

Thus, the first steps for Hispanics, in order to advance themselves in the United States, is to keep this nostalgia in check, otherwise it obscures the reality of the harsh living conditions and brutal poverty of the country from which they hail. It obscures their vision for what could ultimately become a prosperous future for them in the United States. One key element that Latino must keep in mind is that they do not have to reinvent the wheel. All they must do is to study the new host culture, the Anglo-American, or the Anglo-Protestant culture, as it is more commonly referred to, by which they are surrounded, and to notice that which they can adopt from it in order achieve success in the United States.

Chapter Three

Anglo Protestant Culture

Beginning in the 17th century on the east coast of what was to become the United States, there began a new culture started by a group of dissenters whose religious and spiritual views had become unwelcome in their native homeland, England. They felt that God had two groups of human beings on earth, those who were the elect and the non-elect, the latter group doomed to suffer punishment in the after-life. The elect, they felt, were to show their virtue through good works. The Puritan mentality was very much guided by these theological concepts of virtue, salvation, and good works. According to Samuel Huntington (2004),

> "[The Protestants] were, however, generally committed to an emphasis on the individual's direct relation to God, the supremacy of the Bible as a sole source of God's word, salvation through faith and for many the transforming experience of being "born again," personal responsibility to proselytize and bear witness, and democratic and participatory church organization." (p 65)

This would later give rise to the universities of Harvard and Yale. Both institutions were very much grounded in what was to become known as the Protestant ethic. At first it was not so much a "work ethic" so much as it was to become a religious ethic. Gutenberg's press had revolutionized religion in Europe, and the Puritan settlers were no less enthusiastic about reading scripture. This gave them a very scholarly way of viewing the world and the universities were a natural extension of their religious principles. At first the mission of the universities was to propagate the ideals of "hard core" Protestantism. In addition to these collegiate communities, the Puritan ethic condemned showy dress, festivities, and many forms and expressions of merriment. Life for them was to be spent reading scripture, and for the boys at least, a chance to attend one of the universities they had erected. The early American culture was already being shaped by a unique approach to scholarly pursuits and literacy. Cotton Mather was to become one of the most prolific writers of that era, expounding his views on the supernatural and the Salem witchcraft trials. The Puritan experience left an indelible stamp on the American culture that lasted well into the 20th Century. This stamp had, as one of its trademarks, an emphasis on lifelong learning. The other mark left behind by the Puritan experiment was a view of education having an intrinsic value. By intrinsic I mean that the value and benefit of learning was felt to be good for the mind and soul. It was not necessarily meant to be something showy or having only extrinsic or social value. Education, early on, was seen as something that would lead to self-betterment and to human growth. In the centuries to come, this situation had changed slightly. An education was now seen as having a real and viable external, or extrinsic, value in the workplace. This was the result of the increase in specialization following the Industrial Revolution. Certainly no one can doubt that those who possess a college degree have traditionally become the ones who earn higher wages. And there is still a social status attached to having a degree.

Another legacy left behind by the Puritan settlements of New England was an emphasis on social service. Their religious views impelled them to strive to lead a life of virtue, and many times this entailed helping others. This can still be seen in the modern mainstream American culture. After the events of September 11, 2001, there was a renewed call toward service felt within many aspects of American life. This took many expressions. The most obvious, of course, became military service. Other organizations such as the Peace Corps also experienced a renewed sense of mission. Many social service organizations had already been active even before September 11 and had become a part of the legacy of service in America. Others were devoted to national service such as AmeriCorps and Habitat for Humanity. There are numerous other groups that seek to serve Americans in need, such as soup kitchens, religious volunteer youth groups, and hospitals which admit volunteers to donate time to assisting the staff. In the 20th Century, another major movement that stressed service as its goal was the ecology movement. The havoc that was being wreaked by indiscriminate hunting and construction projects, as well as the scientific discovery of a hole in the ozone layer, and the greenhouse effect, helped stimulate this movement. The universities began offering areas of concentration related to this new science. This has become a major form of modern day social service.

The Puritan culture, which later gave rise to the Enlightenment, left another uniquely American trademark: an emphasis on literacy. As mentioned above, the publication of the Bible in English was a major factor in promoting literacy among Protestants in England and in the Colonies. This allowed the Puritans to feel empowered within their faith. God, they felt, was speaking directly to them. A century later, literacy was still being promoted in the Colonies, yet the range of material had expanded as a result of a newfound interest in natural science. Much time was spent among the Puritan elders in reading, analyzing, digesting, and discussing religious tomes. Even to this day, it can be fairly said that more books are freely available to be read and even purchased in the United States than in any other country. To this day, the literacy rate in the United States is much higher than most countries.

With the availability of books has come a new phenomenon in the Anglo Protestant culture: the self-help movement. This movement can be readily traced to the importation of psychology from Europe. Although Sigmund Freud's work had a shaky start in the United States, the movement to understand people's unconscious conflicts through the method of psychoanalysis gained rapid growth in the decades following Freud's death in 1939. Later theorists developed their own unique brands of psychological insight and even different schools of thought in psychology. This later gave rise to a distillation process whereby a very simple and readable form of psychological self-help instruction began to make its way to the general reading public. Psychology was no longer to be found purely as an esoteric and specialized knowledge in the universities. The common man, it was felt, could help himself. Thus by the third quarter of the 20th Century, one could easily purchase a book which could deal with any range of topics relating to one's improvement. Dealing with divorce, making friends, discovering one's sexuality, and dealing with the past were now topics open for everyone to read and explore. This has, curiously, the echo of the Puritan experience in which the common man could read the Bible and experience grace in an individualistic manner. As scripture became available for the common man to own and experience, so psychology became the new scripture in what was becoming a rapidly secularized society. American culture, then, can be safely regarded as one in which the common man is encouraged to better himself through personal growth. The self-help movement reached a cultural zenith during the 1960s when psychoanalysis was in vogue. This was to become yet another example of how a specialized treatment intended for the upper classes in the Victorian era was to become more freely available to the workingman. This all changed with the rise of managed care and the subsequent shrinkage of the middle class in the United States. More common today are the fixed number of sessions with psychologists in a managed care system, and although diluted, may still be of benefit to those who need short-term therapy.

Another Anglo Protestant cultural legacy is regionalism. During the Colonial period, each individual colony developed its own unique set of customs, linguistic variations, regional accents, and political priorities. In the mid-19th Century, the Southern states, which formed the Confederacy, developed their own unique collective, not just as individual states, but also as a group of states. The states in the North that formed the Union had a distinct Yankee heritage, especially the New England states. In both North and South, another form of regionalism developed: the affiliations with universities. Harvard and Yale became bastions of New England culture and others further south, such as Emory University or Tuskegee University, became symbols of Southern life. Out West, the Land Grant Colleges became symbols of the pioneering spirit. To this day, driving on any major highway in any state in the Union, one can always see on license plates and rear windows the names of the alma maters of the drivers. These signs and stickers are more common than any other symbol of affiliation.

During the last three hundred fifty years, university affiliation has become a unique mark of the American character. Without a doubt, this country has produced some of the finest institutions of higher education in the world. Even presidents of Mexico have come to American universities to study political science and economics. From medicine to law, architecture and engineering, the universities in the United States are still offering a premier education to future practitioners in these fields. The quality of the faculty and the size of the endowments from private foundations and corporations have clearly given institutions such as Princeton, Dartmouth, and Stanford a world class reputation. What has made these universities so strong is a fierce commitment to fostering critical thinking and individual thought in the undergraduates. Students are encouraged to truly consider what they are being taught. This once again is a legacy to the fierce intellectualism of the New England Puritans. University affiliations in America are also seen very vividly in NCAA sporting and fundraising events. There is a strong effort made on the part of American universities to receive endowments anywhere from $50 to gifts into the millions. Universities must do this, of course, to remain solvent. It has the effect, however, of cementing ties between graduates and their alma maters. This has the ultimate benefit of allowing one to feel a sense of membership with an institution that has a fine reputation. Abraham Maslow wrote of the need for belonging in his hierarchy of needs. Although he may not have had university alumni associations in mind, these groups nevertheless allow one to feel connected with an institution of high social value.

Another uniquely American trait is the wish to stay healthy and lead a healthy lifestyle. Exercise has become a permanent part of the American landscape. Once again, academia added to this cultural trait. The "common knowledge" that we now find so logical came about as a result of American medical research universities. These schools have provided an invaluable service to the

American public: the findings of medical empirical studies. American universities have produced some of the best and most well controlled studies. These empirical studies have done more to expand humankind's knowledge of a whole range of health related issues, such as the Human Genome Project, HIV prevention, risk factors for heart disease, cancer, diabetes, and a host of other ailments. It has been clearly shown that a regimen of regular exercise and a healthy diet can help to mitigate the onset of various diseases. This gave rise to the health movement, which once again places specialized knowledge from books directly into the hands of the common man. This allows him to have direct control over his destiny, or at least the destiny of his own body. It further highlights the individualistic nature of the American character and the sense of empowerment it can give the common man once he decides to take his foreseeable future into his own hands. Academia helps to shape national culture in a positive way.

This exploration of the Anglo-Protestant culture is meant to give the reader an understanding of how various aspects of a culture can be used for advancement in society. Any minority group in the United States can emulate the proactive, inquisitive, methodical and competitive nature of Anglo-Protestant culture. Specifically, the Latino population can benefit by incorporating the proactive aspect of the Anglo-Protestant culture with regards to their children's elementary and high school education. Latino parents would do their children a great service by taking on an aggressively proactive stance with regards to how well their children are doing in school, how their grades are fluctuating, and meeting with the teachers often. Time after time educators have informed me that Latino parents are very passive with regards to their children's education. They drive the children to school, and pick them up in the afternoon. However, the Latino parents expect the school to be completely in charge of their children's education. It is the *school's* responsibility to educate children they feel, not *theirs*. In the Anglo-Protestant culture, the situation is the opposite. Caucasian parents are partners with the schools. They take a very proactive stance with regard to tutoring, Parent-Teacher conferences, school volunteer activities, and extracurricular activities. Both my parents were very active and I know that this is what allowed me to remain academically strong.

What Latinos parents must realize is that the school system may not do all that is necessary to properly educate a child. Modern teachers are faced with overcrowded classrooms, and in some cases insufficient or outdated materials. Latino parents must take their child's education into their own hands, in the tradition of proactive Anglo-Saxon culture, while still retaining and enjoying their own uniquely Latino cultural heritage. This is Selective Cultural Adoption at its best.

When we study Protestant, or Anglo-American culture, there are several aspects which comprise the culture which we have to keep together in order to maintain a collective sense of what defines the culture. Samuel Huntington (2004) in his book *Who Are We? The Challenges To America's National Identity*, writes,

"America's core culture has been and, at the moment, is still primarily the culture of the seventeenth- and eighteenth-century settlers who founded American society. The central elements of that culture can be defined in a variety of ways but includes the Christian religion, Protestant values and moralism, a work ethic, the English language, British traditions of law, justice, and the limits of government power, and a legacy of European art, literature, philosophy, and music." (p. 40)

According to Huntington, Anglo-Protestant culture has certain central elements, among them: The Dissidence of Dissent, The American Creed, Individualism and the Work Ethic, Moralism and the Reform Ethic.

Throughout much of American history, there have been numerous efforts to get settlers and immigrants to the country to assimilate to a more American Protestant culture. As Huntington (2004) points out, "Throughout American history, people who are not white Anglo-Saxon Protestants have become American by adopting America's Anglo-Protestant culture and political values. This benefited them and the country." (p. 61) These benefits can include, among other things, a shared sense of national unity, and a shared sense of political unity. It can allow for people to feel connected to one another in ways that would not be possible if everyone were to retain their language of national origin. This is self-evident if we have, in any one suburban city block, several houses each of which will contain families of different national origins. For instance, if there is an Italian family living next to a Mexican family that is itself domiciled next to a Chinese family, which is next door to a Laotian family, they will all have a different language and different forms of cultural expression. While no one is advocating the abandonment of a native language a shared usage of the English language and certain cultural American traits can help neighbors feel connected with one another.

Huntington (2004) does a good job of elucidating the components of Anglo-Protestant culture. He wrote,

"The Protestant emphasis on the individual conscience and the responsibilities of the individuals to learn God's truths directly from the Bible promoted American commitment to individualism, equality, and the rights to freedom of religion and opinion. Protestantism stressed the work ethic and the responsibility of the individual for his own success or failure in life. With its congregational forms of church organization, Protestantism fostered opposition to hierarchy and the assumption that similar democratic forms be employed in government. It also promoted moralistic efforts to reform society and to secure peace and justice at home and throughout the world." (p. 68)

I have heard Latinos tell me their opinion that Anglo Americans have no "real" culture. By this, they mean to imply that the absence of a national folkloric dance, or folkloric music, as we have in Hispanic countries, is to deduce that America has no viable culture or traditions. In many countries, in both Latin America and in Europe, there are national holidays and celebrations that mark the date of an important historical event. The traditional music, dancing and costumes that readily identify a national culture accompany these events. A prime example is the Oktoberfest in Germany. Yet, while music, dancing, and national costume are colorful and visible reminders of national cultures, it would be a mistake to assume that because one does not witness those types of events among Anglo Americans, that there is no true American culture. As Huntington (2004), points out, the components of American culture are not to be found in a form of national dance, or folkloric costume. Rather, Anglo American culture is to be found in the beliefs and values quoted above. Ideas such as equality, democracy, religious freedom, a free market economy, and limited government, form the basis of "real" American culture. Latinos are mistaken if they feel that there is a cultural vacuum in the United States that they must impregnate with their music, dancing, and Spanish language.

Chapter Four

Cultural Integration

To become the most effective citizen possible, there are times when one must pick and choose the aspects of any culture that will be instrumental in aiding successful citizenship. In the preceding chapters, I have outlined the basic tenets of Hispanic culture as well as the basic tenets of Anglo Protestant culture. It is my sincerest wish to convey the message that no single culture in this world is superior to any other culture. It is only natural that members of a single ethnic or cultural group will feel that their own cultural heritage is somehow superior in virtue to all others. Anthropologists refer to this process as ethnocentrism. It is the tendency to view the world only through one's own cultural perspective. Certainly the Puritans had their own form of ethnocentrism. This is why they were not able to survive in Holland. They wanted their surroundings to maintain a uniquely English character. Fortunately, there was available land on the eastern shores of North America with which to make a New England. Theirs was a world of scripture, demons, good works, Christian education, and English culture. Later groups were to arrive and transplant their own worldviews from the Old Country into the American diaspora.

Each culture will have its own unique strengths and virtues. I believe it is part of human tendency to feel that one's culture is unique, that it has a set of virtues that no other culture shares. We live in an age when culture is celebrated. We also live in an age where the means of travel to other countries is faster, cheaper, and more readily available than ever before. A New Yorker can conceivably wake up on Friday morning and by Saturday morning eat breakfast in Madrid.

Assimilation in America has become a hotly contested debate. The most powerful and most vivid way in which this debate is being brought to the fore is through the large numbers of immigrants coming into the United States every year. According to Marcelo M. Suarez-Orozco (2000), there are two features of immigration that make the debate salient: the sheer numbers and the shift in demographics in the immigration population. Up until the year 1950, almost 90% of all immigration was being fed by Europe and Canada. Half a century later, over 50% of immigration is from Latin America and 27% is from Asia. The literature that has been written about assimilation and immigration has rested on three premises: Suarez-Orozco refers to them as the "clean break assumption," the "homogeneity" assumption, and the "progress" assumption.

The clean break pattern of immigration could more readily be witnessed from the middle of the 19th century up until the early 20th century. Immigrants who left one country to settle in another made a "clean break." Suarez-Orozco described it thusly: "The norm . . . was that immigrants leaving Ireland or Eastern Europe were not supposed to look back . . . the renaming rituals at Ellis Island, where immigrants traded-some voluntarily, others involuntarily-exotic names for "Americanized versions," signified the beginning of a new life." The second premise became that immigrants would begin to blend in to the mainstream middle class culture. This became known as the "melting pot" paradigm in sociology. The third inherent premise of this model that Suarez-Orozco defines as the "progress assumption" was that there would be a linear increase in economic and educational progress. It was assumed that the infrastructure of Eastern Europe and Britain had on some level failed these immigrants, thus their adoption of the American work and corporate ethics were thought to elevate their status to a level that had heretofore not existed in their countries of origin. As the author wrote, ". . . a coherent narrative unfolds: as immigrants give up their old ways, they assimilate to middle class, white, European American Protestant culture, [and] they find enormous rewards." What allowed the clean break model to work was the fact that the transportation systems, especially airline flight and electronic communication, both of which are taken for granted, simply did not exist back then. A transatlantic voyage was not just a means of transportation; for many of these immigrants that transoceanic trip became a symbol. They were headed towards a new life. The hazards and enormous costs which no doubt depleted a family's coffers as well as their physical energy made the transatlantic voyage an absolute.

Modern transportation systems as well as the closeness and uninterrupted landscape separating Latin America from the United States, has made immigration and assimilation an entirely different phenomenon. Suarez-Orozco (2000) points out that this has now allowed people to immigrate to Latin America in an uninterrupted "flow" rather than the "waves" of the previous two centuries. The bi-product of this form of immigration is that it, in his words, "replenishes" the cultural heritages of the countries of origin from which these immigrants came. The older pattern of immigration caused the assimilation process to follow a natural progression whereby over several generations the cultural heritage of the original migrants was all but forgotten and a new life was begun. The new continuous pattern of immigration, especially from Latin American, allows the new flow of immigrants to replenish what would otherwise be a receding cultural trademark on the landscape of the United States. Thus, ease of transportation, the Internet, long-distance calling cards, and a generous immigration policy have allowed foreign culture to flow in and assimilation *to flow out*. What is also *flowing out* is money, back into the countries of origin. As Suarez-Orozco noted, "with international remittances estimated at nearly $100,000,000,000 per annum, immigration remittances and investments have become vital to the economies of most countries of emigration." What is also *flowing out* is political influence. The last Dominican presidential election was affected by Dominicans not in the Dominican Republic but by New York City. Dominicans comprise the largest population of recent arrivals in New York City. In a similar vein, candidates in Mexico have begun to utilize the instrumental value of the 7,000,000 Mexican immigrants living in America. The ability of Mexican immigrants to maintain what amounts to two nationalities has allowed many Mexican immigrants to maintain an active voice in politics with their compatriots who reside in Mexico. As the author put it, "immigrants today are more likely to be at once "here and there," articulating dual consciousness and dual identities."

Unfortunately, a corollary to this pattern of immigration has been to create a highly stratified infrastructure in American society. Suarez-Orozco (2000) has characterized the American economy to be operating like an "hourglass." At the top of the hourglass lie the people who work in the "well-remunerated, knowledge-intensive economic sphere" which is linked to the technological, information-based sectors of the economy. On the other end of the hourglass, the large, rounded bottom, lie the people with few employable skills and low educational status. As Suarez-Orozco notes: ". . . in the new economy there are virtually no bridges from those at the bottom of the hourglass to move into the more desirable sectors . . . the kinds of jobs typically available today to low-skilled new immigrants do not offer serious prospects of upward mobility."

As stated earlier, the patterns of migration from the mid-19th century to the early 20th century were very different from the pattern of migration from Mexico. The main difference being that the United States shares the contiguous border with Mexico, whereas earlier migration patterns took place across a transatlantic voyage. Furthermore, the nations that were sending immigrants to America were not sending national flags and their literature along with the immigrants. The current pattern of immigration from Mexico is sending out not only large numbers of immigrants, but a wholesale transplantation of their culture as well.

However, this situation is not entirely one-sided. There is evidence that the push for assimilation and integration is already taking place. Fonte and Barone (2000), in *The American Enterprise* magazine, referenced research made by Public Agenda, which found that citizens in the United States today are fully supportive of patriotic assimilation. They found that 87 percent of immigrant parents and 88 percent of all parents agreed with the statement, "Schools should make a special effort to teach new immigrants about American values." In this study, parents were asked to choose between two statements. One was whether schools should be "instilling pride in [students'] ethnic group's identity and heritage," or whether the schools should make an effort to help students ". . . be proud of being part of this country and learn[ing] the rights and responsibilities of citizenship." Fully 79 percent of parents from all ethnic extractions chose pride in America. In the same vein, 87 percent of Hispanic parents also preferred "pride in America" to "pride in one's ethnic heritage." The same study found that 65 percent of Anglo-American respondents felt that schools should "help new immigrants absorb America's language and culture as quickly as possible even if their native language and culture are neglected." The passage of Proposition 209 and 227 in California and I-200 in the state of Washington point to an emerging consensus that cultural integration of minorities will ultimately be in their best favor.

In February 1998, at the Los Angeles Coliseum, over 91,000 soccer fans attended the Gold Cup soccer match between the Mexican and the United States teams. The Latinos heckled the Star-Spangled Banner, and then threw cans, bottles, and food at the players on the American team. A Mexican-American soccer fan later described how these belligerent Latinos doused him and his young son with soda and beer because he was displaying a small American flag. One of the soccer players on the American team recalled that he had received better treatment in Mexico City than in Los Angeles, California. Is this part of a disturbing trend? The question becomes: Why does this happen? What causes such antipathy to be expressed by Latinos towards the United States? This country has given Latinos jobs, food stamps, welfare assistance, medical care, the opportunity to vote, and the opportunity to travel back and forth between our borders and other countries. So, why are they biting the hand that feeds their mouths?

There is a bumper sticker that some people have used to adorn their cars, and it reads: "America: Love It or Leave It." This is a somewhat harsh and blunt way of expressing patriotic citizenship. Nevertheless, a point ought to be made that in order to lead a contented and productive existence in the United States, one will profit from an affinity for and an allegiance to, the

American landscape. This is not to say that one must always love everything about a national culture. It is nigh impossible to be completely enamored of every single aspect of any single country's culture. I find myself rejecting aspects of American culture that do not suit me. The glorified depiction of violence in movies, the obsession with sex in the media, and an all-pervasive consumerism would most likely be my top three targets that I personally reject of American culture. Violent images on television, in music videos on MTV, and in motion pictures have all promoted a culture of violence. The rap music industry likewise glorifies the life of gangsters. The widespread availability of handguns has been one of the easiest ways to maintain a culture of violence. To watch so much gratuitous violence desensitizes the mind and bankrupts the soul. Likewise, to present sex as a sport or as a cheap voyeuristic thrill bereft of feelings or even spiritual qualities can have a degrading effect upon the human spirit. All the while, discussion of the serious topics of birth control, the lifelong consequences of having a baby, the economic burden of raising a family, and other, even more private and sensitive topics such as abortion and masturbation are avoided.

The purpose here is not to promote a wholesale love affair with all things American. Each one of us must make a choice as to what we will adopt and what we will reject. However, what occurred at the Los Angeles Coliseum in 1998 was not an example of patriotic American citizenship. It was an outright wholesale and bigoted attack on an innocent American sports team, but what is even more troubling is the fact that it was an outright cultural attack on America itself.

Where does the anger come from? Is it based on history? The changes and shifts in borders between countries is a fact of life. The land mass of the southern half of California, Arizona, New Mexico and Texas, as well as other areas, may have once belonged to the Republic of Mexico, and ceded after the Treaty of Hidalgo, but as the saying goes, "that's history." It's over. There is no way that Mexico could possibly retake this land. It may have been repopulated with Mexicans but it has been and is now a permanent part of the American landscape. Furthermore, there is something that Mexicans continuously forget when they bemoan the reacquisition of the Southwestern lands; there were very few Mexicans there to begin with. Victor Davis Hanson (2003) chronicles the state of affairs at the time of acquisition:

> ". . . when the United States stole California there were fewer than 10,000 Mexicans living in a vast uninhabited area, one that itself had been stolen from Spain, which in turn had stolen it from the Indians . . . Look at a . . . text and you see the map of the original Nuevo California that includes not just the present-day state, but all of Nevada, Arizona, Utah, parts of New Mexico, Colorado and even southern Wyoming!–as if there were once thousands of prosperous Mexicans plying their culture in a vast Hispanic American North." (p. 32)

The political movement to retake the land has a dreamy appeal to Latinos, but it will never be more than a dream. This is analogous to the current situation in Palestine. Jewish settlements have been made in the Gaza Strip; however, complete Jewish ownership of the land is nearly impossible. Some sociologists have viewed the current situation in the United States as a passive cultural takeover that's happening rather than the traditional militaristic acquisition of land that takes place between two countries. From a certain point of view an argument could be made that Latinos have won back this land. This may not have been a planned takeover, as one would expect in a military operation. The process of migrating legally and illegally, having large families, and importing Mexican culture have all played a role in turning the Southwest into an extension of Mexico. I do not believe that Mexicans masterminded this tactic. That is to say, I do not believe this was part of a grand scheme to retake the land through re-population and importation of culture. But this is precisely what has happened. There are hostile military takeovers and there are passive cultural takeovers. Yet this will all serve to sour relations between the United States and Mexico. In America, it will inevitably cause resentment against Latin America in general and Mexico in particular. Samuel Huntington (2004) describes a possible rise in white nativism in the American cultural landscape in the not-so-distant future. As he wrote,

". . . a plausible reaction to the demographic changes underway in the United States could be the rise of an anti-Hispanic, anti-black, and anti-immigrant movement composed largely of white, working- and middle-class males, protesting their job losses to immigrants and foreign countries, the perversion of their culture, and the displacement of their language. Such a movement can be labeled, 'white nativism.'" (p. 310)

He also references Carol Swain's 2002 book, *The New White Nationalism in America*, who wrote, "cultured, intelligent, and often possessing impressive degrees from some of America's premier colleges and universities, this new breed of white racial advocate is a far cry from the populist politicians and hooded Klansmen of the Old South". Her book describes this new cadre of nationalists not as the lovers of eugenics and Social Darwinism that was seen in the 1930s. Rather, this is a group advocating ethnic preservation in the face of immigrant onslaught who believe that race produces culture. These nationalists believe that the slow but definite changes taking place will spell the substitution of Anglo culture by black or Latino, which are seen as morally and intellectually inferior. Somewhat dismally, Swain predicts that the United States is "increasingly at risk of large-scale racial conflict unprecedented in our nation's history." What underlies all of this current and predicted tension is economic and job-related competition. Any time there are two individuals, two groups, or even two nations and a limited number of jobs as well as a finite amount of land, there will be tensions between the competitors. This was shown dramatically in pre-war Germany. The worldwide Great Depression had caused the German Mark to become so devalued people were actually burning cartloads of them instead of firewood. It was felt Jewish banking and Marxist economic entities were conspiring to keep the Germans in a state of perpetual victimhood after the Treaty of Versailles. What made Hitler's message so appealing for the German people was his call for Germans to retake their motherland and claim it in the name of the German race.

I am confident that this will never happen in the United States. I believe that Americans are inherently moral, caring and open-minded people. That's not to say that racial violence has not occurred in the United States, but the advantage in this country is that there is a built-in safeguard in American culture: the ability to learn from mistakes. This country is in a stage of continuous evolution, not just from the history of our own nation but also from the histories of other nations of the world. Americans are a very forward-looking people and the least likely to repeat the mistakes from the past. The whole world was witness to the atrocities of Nazi Germany and of Communist Russia under Stalin. America would never retreat to a political system or structure which history and wars have proven to be disastrous. To even entertain the notion that a fascist regime could rise up in the United States would be to overlook one of the most obvious and enduring principles which Americans hold dear: democracy. Regimes have risen and been snuffed out in countries which are not used to American-style democracy. That is why we have a bicameral system of government; it is the fail-safe design envisioned by the founders of the fledgling American Republic. The President of the United States must await the approval of Congress before many actions may take place, and new laws which are passed are under continuous scrutiny by the Supreme Court. Germany had no such system of government in place when Adolph Hitler manipulated his way into office as Chancellor. He completely revamped the government. In the United States there is no higher law than the Constitution of the United States. And I do not foresee any amendments to be passed which would modify the inherent principles in that document. If one examines the histories of most nations in Europe, one sees that there is hardly a single nation that has managed to retain its system of government for more than a century. On the other hand, the executive, legislative, and judicial branches of the American government have remained relatively unchanged since the ratification of the U.S. Constitution in 1788. Of course, the United States endured a major civil war that tore the country in half. Robert E. Lee, as Commander of the Confederate armies, became in a sense an enemy of the State. Jefferson Davis from Mississippi and Alexander Stephens from Georgia were elected President and Vice-President, respectively, of the Confederate States of America. On March 11, 1861, the Confederate States of America ratified their own constitution. This sundering became a gaping wound in the New Republic. The United States is not without its own disruptive history, yet democracy prevailed. The Confederate States were re-absorbed into the Union and the original Colonial Constitution again became the primary document that would guide and sustain the Federal government.

In order for the ideals set forth in our national ethos to prevail and in order for the American Republic, as it now stands, to function all groups must once again see themselves as part of a national order. What happened in the Los Angeles Coliseum in 1998 was a glaring example of cultural separatism at its worst. In a sense, the soft-heartedness of Federal and State agencies in allowing immigrants to use their native language by staffing their offices with multi-lingual staff has allowed this multi-cultural separatism to flourish. The presence of many languages in this country has done more to cause fellow citizens to feel alienated from each other than perhaps any other cultural element. As Huntington (2004) wrote,

> "A persuasive case can be made that, in a shrinking world, all Americans should know at least one important foreign language-Chinese, Japanese, Hindi, Russian, Arabic, Urdu, French, German, or Spanish-so as to understand a foreign culture and communicate with its people. It is quite different to argue that Americans should know a non-English language in order to communicate with their fellow citizens." (p. 321)

Huntington himself quotes the late California senator S. I. Hayakawa, who said: ". . . Hispanics alone have maintained there is a problem. There [has been] considerable movement to make Spanish the second official language."

In May of 2002, I joined the Peace Corps and was sent overseas to the Republic of Moldova. It is one of the newer countries formed after the dissolution of the Soviet Union. It lies between Romania and Ukraine. The Peace Corps informed me that Romanian is the official language and that I would be required to take Romanian language lessons in Moldova. Even before I left, I was already listening to Romanian language cassettes and attempting to absorb as many Romanian words so as to have an advantage. When we arrived, not only did we feel the anticipated, and normal, expectation to speak Romanian, but also we eagerly began our Romanian language lessons nearly every day of our three-month training period. There was almost an unspoken competition among the volunteers to see who could speak it the best. We would show off our nascent Romanian vocabulary to each other even when we were not in the company of Moldovan nationals. It was a testament to our ambition, our eagerness to fit in and be accepted. Quite understandably, the

Moldovan government expected us to blend in to society by learning their language and culture. We saw this training and deployment of language skills and cultural knowledge as *de rigueur.* My role was to be an English language instructor. And the other volunteers were assigned to either health or agricultural volunteer posts. It was an all or nothing proposition. The Peace Corps as well as the Moldovan government and citizens expected us to fit in by knowing passable Romanian and learning Moldovan customs. Even after I returned, I continued to study Romanian. This is in stark contrast to the current situation in which the American government, as well as State and local offices, in their eagerness to welcome foreigners and to keep society running smoothly, now have documents and forms in a variety of languages. These municipal offices ask little or no effort to be made on the part of foreign people coming to the United States to accommodate themselves with English or knowledge of American customs. In a sense there is a very subtle political hypocrisy occurring within the different levels of the American government. It expects Peace Corps volunteers to make every effort to be trained in the language, customs, and culture of the host country to which it sends its volunteers. Furthermore, if any Peace Corps volunteer in any way disrespects a host country's nationals or breaks any law while in service, that volunteer is in real danger of being sent back to the States. However, the United States government does not hold foreign immigrants accountable to the standards to which it holds the Peace Corps volunteers. In my view, that which is expected of American citizens serving in the Peace Corps or any other Federal agency should be expected of those who enter our borders. Those who come to the United States should be held to the same linguistic and cultural expectations as those that America sends overseas to serve in a government post.

Chapter Five

Historical Assimilation

What does it mean to assimilate? What does it mean to integrate? In the natural world, there are many species of animals that use camouflage and other tactics in order to blend in with their environment and thus avoid predation. An animal's ability to make itself indistinguishable from its immediate natural environment has an obvious adaptive survival value. Of course, human society does not function like the societies of the natural world. If a person does not blend in with his environment, there is no predator ready to devour him.

So why is there so much focus in social science and political science on assimilation, acculturation, and integration? After all, do we not live in a multicultural society that celebrates diversity? Are we not the most progressive-minded democracy on earth? Have we not made great strides to improve civil rights, end discrimination, and ensure fair practices in employment and in society? In our society, we have norms, customs, traditions, and social expectations. Although this is not in any way a hostile environment, such as can be seen in an African savannah, we nevertheless have a way of life firmly established in our society. In Darwinian terms, only the fittest will survive. What do we mean when we say, "fittest?" By fittest, we can take this to mean only those individuals who have the skills, capacities, abilities, and sensibilities that are highly compatible with American society. We can also take this to mean a person having a "good fit" between himself, herself, and society. Basically, these two concepts are one. Someone who has the skills and abilities valued by American society is also the person who has a good fit *for* society. For more than 300 years in America different groups have come to these shores and imported their own unique skills and strengths. They have all, to some extent or another enriched the American landscape. However, the rate of this process of integrating and importing of abilities has taken place at different tempos. A brief examination of American immigration will make this clear. Fonte and Barone (2000), in *The American Enterprise* magazine, documented the rate of immigration and subsequent assimilation.

The Irish, as he documented, were the first large post-Revolutionary group to migrate to America. In the 1840s, after the great potato famine struck Ireland, 700,000 Irish nationals immigrated to America. A decade later, in the 1850s, one million Irish nationals migrated to the United States. In the period between 1860 and 1914, the Irish populations in the United States increased again by 2.4 million. For these Irish men and women, their Catholicism was their religious mainstay. This of course went contrary to the Protestant culture of the Northeast, and as Fonte and Barone (2000) documented, their predilection for "statism" and social hierarchy caused many to become policemen. They faced discrimination from the outside. They were referred to as the "wild Irish," which may have stemmed from the high rates at that time of alcoholism and crime. Irish uniqueness began to manifest itself in the political arena. They began to identify themselves with the national Democratic Party. This was seen as the party that was more sympathetic to the poor working-man and more involved with civil rights. This may have stemmed also from their Roman Catholicism. The Roman Catholic Church, as a large and powerful institution, has a state-like quality inherent in its hierarchy. The roots in Roman Catholicism may explain Irish bias towards the Democratic Party. Both are large, and have a state-like appeal to the Irish. The government is supposed to ensure civil rights, eliminate poverty, and maintain social programs. The Catholic Church has also established numerous charities. Thus, the Irish may have more easily gravitated to a political party that had a state-like program inherent in its ethos and platform. So to be Irish meant that one was Irish-Catholic, and if one was Irish-Catholic, one was also a Democrat. A similar case will be made later about the Latino culture.

This religious-political orientation culminated with the inauguration of John F. Kennedy as President of the United States in 1960. The appointing of Robert Kennedy as Attorney General doubled the family's influence. Even then, there was still widespread anxiety that they would follow the dictates of Rome rather than the Constitution. However, this represented a huge step for Irish-Catholics to become the "movers and shakers" in American society. As Fonte and Barone (2000) documented, intermarriage became more accepted and the availability of contraception shrunk the size of the Irish-Catholic family. In his words, "the Irish became woven into the fabric of American life. It took 120 years."

African-Americans have faced a similar uphill battle to become integrated and successful in American society. Their predecessors of course came much earlier and under more corruptible circumstances than that of the Irish famine. The first slaves to set foot upon America were those who were brought to

Jamestown in 1619. However, in Fonte and Barone's (2000) view, it was not so much the arrival of the slaves from Africa that was pivotal, rather, the migration of black Americans into the cities above the Mason-Dixon Line. In the North, blacks enjoyed few privileges; however, as Fonte and Barone documents, politics, unions, and civil service became their avenues of influence. They also became talented entertainers, athletes, and musicians. Blacks were also exhibiting, like their Irish cohorts, alcoholism and high crime rates. The blacks also incited inner city riots unparalleled since the Irish protested the draft in 1863 in New York. The decade between 1965 and 1975 saw a large increase in crime and offenses, half of which were committed by blacks. And there were many blacks on welfare. However, like the Irish, blacks began to take their cause to the voting booth to effect change. In 1956, Adam Clayton Powell supported President Eisenhower, and in 1960, nearly two-thirds of blacks voted for John Kennedy. As Fonte and Barone documented, the blacks began to exhibit a similar voting pattern to the Irish. In 1964, black voting tended to be heavily biased toward the Left. Bobby Kennedy and Lyndon Johnson had large appeal for blacks based on their civil rights causes. This contrasted with Barry Goldwater's move against civil rights. Black voters endorsed the idea of an expanded government and its role in society. However, what they may not have realized is that their progress in jobs, pay rate, and education throughout the 1950s and 60s was occurring without the benefit of large federal help. Now, black families' incomes are almost equivalent to those of white families. There are now a number of black colleges in the South offering a quality education to those who are accepted. The nomination of former Secretary of State Colin Powell, as well as Condoleeza Rice as the current Secretary of State, has further proven that African-Americans have come into their own in American society. It took 300 years.

The other large group to make a vivid impression upon the American scene was the Italians. Before 1880, there were only 70,000 Italians in America. By 1900, 807,000 more arrived. Between 1900 and 1914, three million more arrived. According to Fonte and Barone (2000), almost 80 percent hailed from Southern Italy. That part of the country was overrun with organized crime, bureaucracies that were not effective, and a stagnant economy. The majority of these immigrants settled in New York City. To this day, nearly half of all Italian Americans are domiciled within one hundred miles of New York City. They formed their own enclave, "Little Italy," and these "urban villagers" were employed as manual laborers, barbers, shoemakers, stonemasons, and shopkeepers. As Fonte and Barone documented, many of these Italian Americans would find work through a *padrone*, who served as a headhunter who found many of these laborers employment for a fee. However, the Italians began to show a different pattern of social preferences than the Irish. The Italians did not show any trust in any major American institution. They also distrusted the schools. This led to a high dropout rate. This became so widespread that many lived by an Italian proverb which stated, "Stupid is he who makes his children better than himself." They also did not show an interest in politics. However, the process of assimilation began to sweep Italians into the American fold. Fonte and Barone documented that service in World War II became a way toward upward mobility through the GI Bill. College admissions climbed from 15 percent in 1940 to 38 percent in 1960. They continued to rise in society and began to move out from their Manhattan nucleus to the suburbs of New York. Their affiliation with the Catholic Church became stronger, and in 1960 Italian Americans voted for John F. Kennedy in higher numbers than the Irish Americans. As Fonte and Barone wrote, ". . . by the 1970s, Italians were thoroughly absorbed into American Life. It took 100 years."

The other major group to leave a lasting impression on American society was the Jews. In 1880, there were 250,000 German Jews living in the United States. This was followed by a large wave of orthodox Jews who spoke Yiddish from the countries of Eastern Europe. In a 30-year time span, from 1885 to 1914, roughly 750,000 Russian Jews arrived. This was supplemented by one million more fleeing the Austro-Hungarian Empire at the outbreak of World War I. After the Armistice, another 400,000 emigrated between 1920 and 1924. Politically these Jews established their own unique view of the State. According to Fonte and Barone (2000), many of these Jews became socialists. The writings of Karl Marx allowed the Jews to feel vindication as non-Christians and to align themselves with non-Jews as part of the proletariat. By 1920, roughly half of the Jews who had migrated to America lived in New York City. They, like the Italians, worked as manual laborers. However, they also began to show an entrepreneurial drive and established successful businesses. Crime and alcoholism were very low in this population. Yet with this upward climb in society, there was still distrust among the Jews of both the Democratic Party and the Republican Party. Between the 1920s and the 1950s, politicians vied for Jewish votes on both the left and right side of the political spectrum. Ideologically, the Jews identified with the Left. They have become, by and large, aligned with the Democratic Party. In addition, there is also a high rate of intermarriage between Jews and non-Jews, which, according to Fonte and Barone's estimate, is over 50 percent. This has led some Jewish Americans to become concerned that they are losing their culture due to this intermarriage and very small families.

Another group to leave a lasting impression has been the Asian immigrants. The Chinese were the first major Asian group to arrive in the United States. Laborers from China were imported in large numbers after the Gold Rush of

1849 in California. They comprised nearly 10 percent of California's population between the decade of 1870 and 1880. Politically, however, they were not a welcome group. This became expressed in the Chinese Exclusion Act of 1882. In the years between 1884 and 1906, 300,000 Japanese nationals came to California and Hawaii to work as laborers in the agriculture industries. In 1924, legislation was passed which effectively ended immigration for Asians completely. There was an allowance, however, for Philippinos to migrate from the American protected territories. It was not until the last few decades of the 20th Century that Asian immigration began to increase. With the passage of the Immigration Act of 1985, large numbers of Asian immigrants began to arrive. Between 1981 and 1996, 4.7 million Asians arrived in the United States. In 1998, Asians and Pacific Islanders comprised a total of 4 percent of our national population. This translated into ten million Asians. In California, they comprise 14 percent of the population. As Fonte and Barone (2000) points out, many of these Asian families immigrated to the United States with an inherent drive for education. They have also demonstrated a very strong entrepreneurial ambition. Interestingly, they differ from their Jewish, Italian, and Irish cohorts. Asian by and large do not favor statism, and this has led to a tendency among some Asian groups, especially the Vietnamese and Koreans, to vote Republican on the basis of being highly anti-communist.

In more recent times, the biggest group to immigrate to the United States has been Latin Americans. Between 1910 and 1930, 700,000 Mexican nationals arrived seeking refuge from the effects of the Mexican Revolution. Between the years 1959 and 1996, more than 800,000 Cubans escaped the Castro regime. Fonte and Barone (2000) estimated that in the 35-year period between the years 1961 and 1996, Latin American immigration reached 8.5 million. The immigration from Mexico nearly quadrupled from the 1960s to the 1990s. By 1998, the grand total was figured to be 30 million in the United States. Latin American immigration has tended to cluster around major American cities. New York City is now the home to large numbers of Puerto Ricans and Dominicans. New Jersey and Florida hold large numbers of Cubans. California, Texas, Illinois, and New York have large concentrations of Mexican Americans. The head count in California in 1998 showed that 31 percent of the population was Latino. Texas showed a 30 percent Latino population. Like many of the Irish and Italian immigrants in the early decades of the 20th Century, Latino immigrants have likewise tended towards manual labor. This would not present a problem for Latinos were it not for the fact that our society is now moving towards an information-based economy. Additionally, Latino income per person was estimated to be only 50 percent of the national average in 1994. The problem lies in the fact that the jobs that Latinos are fill-ing require little education and present little upward mobility. This is why one can readily find Latinos working in the restaurant industry, as hotel cleaning staff, in farm labor, and the like. As Fonte and Barone wrote, "Latino immigrant families put more trust in work than college degrees." This is the point at which many educators and social scientists have begun to question the role of bilingual education for Latinos. The less Latinos know and speak English, the less chance they will have of upward mobility. It is precisely those Latinos who do not know English who are the most exploited and overworked in our economy. It is also those who are the least educated who become subject to these inhumane working conditions. As long as Latino education lags behind the levels required to attain information- and technology-based jobs, the situation is likely to remain dismal for Latinos.

The cultural resistance that Hispanics are displaying against the acquisition of the English language will only serve to keep them from achieving parity with other mainstream groups in the United States. Sadly, Hispanics are not only keeping themselves from achieving parity in English acquisition with mainstream Americans, they are also keeping themselves from achieving parity in English proficiency with other minorities. According to Huntington (2004),

> "Bilingual education has been a euphemism for teaching students in Spanish and immersing them in Spanish culture. The children of past generations of immigrants did not have such programs, became fluent in English and absorbed America's culture. The children of contemporary non-Hispanic immigrants by and large learned English and assimilate into American society faster than those of Hispanic immigrants. Quite apart from the controversies over its impact on students' academic progress, bilingual education has clearly had a negative impact on the integration of Hispanic students into American society." (p. 320–321)

This stubborn resistance to learn English is, in a very real sense, something of a mystery. There almost seems to be a resistance to learning English that goes straight down to the level of the DNA in Hispanics. Yet, the core reasons are, in the end, not very important if one sees the acquisition of English and academic competence as the key to success for Hispanics in the United States. Unfortunately, what has impeded this progress toward the successful acquisition of English among Hispanics has been the strength and persistence of bilingual education. Huntington (2004), quoted a study performed in New York which found that "ninety percent of the students in Spanish bilingual programs failed to make it into mainstream classes after three years, as guidelines stipulate they should." (p. 320) Huntington references an article in the *New York Times* in which a middle school teacher reported, ". . . these kids go home and speak Spanish; they watch TV and listen to music in Spanish; they go to the doctor, and the doctor speaks Spanish." The columnist for the *Times* further reported, "Spanish speaking children don't ever have to break out of their enclosed world: New York has high schools that are virtually all Spanish and even a bilingual community college. Only when students leave school do they discover that their English isn't up to the demands of the job market." (p. 320)

Thus, bilingual education coupled with Spanish-speaking neighborhood enclaves has truly crippled Hispanics' ability to successfully adapt themselves to American society. However, the damage has been done not only in the bilingual education programs of grade schools, it has also extended all the way up to the university level. Ever since the late sixties and early seventies, university departments have established courses in ethnic minority studies as part of their requirements. These ethnic studies departments and their courses were intended to be countermeasures to what was perceived as the evil-Anglo-colonial-imperialistic culture, which had dominated the world for so long. The job of these educators was to provide a series of courses that more and more became politicized and less academic in their focus and instead, became mere factories of anti-white reverse discrimination. Huntington (2004) quotes Arthur Schlesinger who said "A number of institutions . . . require courses in Third World or ethnic studies but not in Western civilization. The mood is one of divesting Americans of the sinful European inheritance and seeking redemptive infusions from non-Western cultures." (p. 175) Thus, what is occurring is cultural entrenchment at three levels of society: the ethnic *barrios*, the bilingual schools, and the embattled and heavily politicized university departments which teach courses which ultimately serve to produce reverse racism and angry grievances for past mistakes which should be, by now, long forgotten. That is to say, a history book nowadays will be only too happy to show the evil European conquest of the New World, however, scant mention will be made of the Aztecs' domination of weaker tribes in the Americas. Or, it will describe the evil conquest of the American Southwest after the Treaty of Hidalgo but little mention will be made of the fact that Mexico stole that land from Spain who in turn had stolen it from the Native Americans.

Ironically, Hispanics have tended to be the ones who have opposed certain bilingual education programs. Huntington (2004) reported a 1997 poll taken in Orange County, California, which found that 83 percent of Hispanic parents favored immediate English instruction as soon as their children began school. He cited a different poll taken in 1997 in the *Los Angeles Times* which found that 84 percent of Latinos in California said they were in support of limits on bilingual education (p. 170). The additional factor which, of course, will be playing a very large role in this slow process of getting Hispanics to learn English, is immigration. The continuous flow upward of immigrants into the United States from Latin America and predominantly Mexico has created the neighborhood enclaves and given rise to a large Spanish-speaking subculture in the United States. In a sense, Hispanics are not being given a chance to assimilate given the fact that their numbers continue to swell each year, due to their continuous influx into the United States. In a way, immigration into the United States and language and cultural assimilation can be compared to the metaphor of a house with a leaky roof. Typically, when there is a leak in the roof, water will trickle into the home, and one ends up with a wet floor. However, if there are several holes in the roof and is pouring rain, one never really gets the chance to completely dry the floor because there is always a new leak allowing water to drip onto the floor. Thus, the house can be the metaphor for the United States and the leaky roof is our leaky border with Mexico. As long as immigration pours through our 'roof' it will be impossible to dry the floor, and completely assimilate immigrants into the United States. At times, it may be useful to consult with other Hispanics to see how they view these cultural liabilities evidenced by Hispanics. Huntington (2004) quoted Lionel Sosa, who listed several Latino cultural characteristics that have retarded their eventual assimilation into society: ". . . mistrust of people outside the family; lack of initiative, self-reliance, and ambition; low priority for education; acceptance of poverty as a virtue necessary for entry into heaven." (p. 254) As Huntington himself reports, "In the meantime, the high level of immigration from Mexico sustains and reinforces among Mexican Americans the Mexican values which are the primary source of their lagging educational and economic progress and slow assimilation into American society." (p. 254)

How will American society ultimately adjust to the realities of the shifting ethnic demographics of the United States? Carol M. Swain (2002), outlined three ways in which the citizenry of the United States will ultimately deal with this issue:

> ". . . the white majority appears to be left with only three clear-cut alternatives for dealing with the broad demographic changes: accepting a new American melting pot, heeding the call of white nationalism and organizing and pressuring government to slow the tide of immigration, or self-segregating by moving into whiter areas of the country." (p. 85)

As she points out, "Fleeing are those working-class whites who cannot afford to live in gated communities or send their children to private schools. In other words, those in direct economic competition with nonwhites are the ones moving most rapidly to whiter states. Almost naturally, a partitioning of the country is occurring as groups self-segregate." (p. 88) This does not portend well with a nation such as ours that prides itself on its inclusiveness of all cultural groups.

Chapter Six

Support Systems in
the Home & Community

The role of support systems in fostering an academically competitive child cannot be over-emphasized. It is common for Hispanic parents to feel that it is the school's job to educate their child. There is an element of passivity in the Hispanic culture that is working against Latinos, especially in the education of young people. In Latin America, there is a long-standing, almost colonial, deference to authority figures. This may have roots in the caste system implemented by Medieval Spain, with its inherent hierarchy, and tight control over the land by barons. This may have left in Latinos an almost permanent stamp of deference to people in authority. The influence of titles and nobility in Latin American may have done more harm than good. However, in 2004, one can see the vestiges of this deference to authority in the way that Latino parents defer to the public school system. They want the teachers to do all the work in educating their children. The Latino parents feel that once a child comes home from school, no further effort needs to be done on their part to expand their child's mind.

Steve Woda, a school psychologist in Los Angeles, reported that the parents under the auspices of the educational community whom he serves feel that it is entirely the school's responsibility to make the child academically competent. However, research shows that whatever skills, both academically and socially, the child gains at school must be dovetailed with an equally structured and disciplined environment at home. For instance, if one is a parent of a student, one should notice whether the child has an appropriate study area that is free from noise, music, and other distractions. In addition, does the child have a set study time? Are there books at home that the child can read? Does the child see his or her parents reading books? Something more substantial than Danielle Steele? A growing child will internalize the messages that are transmitted through the parents' actions and inactions. A young boy witnessing domestic violence will internalize the message that it is normal or somehow appropriate. Likewise, a young girl witnessing her mother withstanding abuse will also internalize the message that this is the kind of behavior that she should one day withstand. The same can be said for alcoholism and drug usage. However, the child who witnesses his parents relate to each other with love and respect and caring will grow up and have a higher likelihood of emulating that behavior. In the same vein, if a child watches his parents read quality books and value learning, it stands to reason that he or she will also value education. William Raspberry wrote in the *Washington Post* (2003) in an article called "An Attitude Gap," that the disparity in academic achievement between whites and blacks has ". . . less and less to do with racism and more and more to do with the habits and attitudes we inculcate among our children." He does not, even for a moment, feel that the academic difference is merely laziness on the part of African Americans. Not at all. However, he does maintain that the attitude towards learning can go a long way towards closing that gap. He quotes Abigail and Stephan Thernstrom in their book "No Excuses: Closing the Racial Gap in Learning" (2003). In the book the Thernstroms make the argument that black families are supportive of education but see good grades in middle school and high school as merely the royal road to college and good jobs. Yet, the authors maintain, if that is the approach to good grades, then the students may as well do the least amount of work in order to get the grades and marks that are barely enough to qualify for that royal road. The Thernstroms contrast this with the environment found in Caucasian and Asian homes. In these homes, one finds a greater number of books. It may not be the case that all these books are read to completion, however, it reflects the culture of learning present in these homes. The Thernstroms also point out the high levels of time spent watching TV in minority homes as compared to the high achieving families. The authors do not question the legacy of racism in becoming part of the equation of the achievement gap. However, they feel that the effect of racism at this point can no longer be used as an adequate reason or excuse to justify underachievement. Historical wrongs should not be forgotten, but the book makes a good point to state that history does not necessarily dictate the future. Raspberry ends his editorial by asking the question, "how do we best use our intellectual, political and moral capital-priming our children for success, or merely supplying them with excuses for failure?"

If any group feels that they are exempt from any kind of expectations to achieve as a result of a beleaguered status, apathy can result. These historical examples are related to parental expectations in that the culture of the home will reflect the larger social culture of which one is a part. Thus, if a Japanese mother and father are raising a child in California, they can take either one of two directions. As a result of Japan's defeat in World War II, and as a result of facing discrimination and internment camps in California after Pearl Harbor, the parents could easily come to feel apathy regarding their child's education. Or, they can liberate themselves from an unpleasant past and feel that they, as parents, are in control of their child's destiny. Once liberated from historical precedents, parents of any ethnic group can begin to feel more empowered to shape and control their child's education. Again, this is not to state that there are not current societal injustices, yet they must be put in their proper perspective. *Geographic boundaries, national borders, and historical wrongdoings did not prevent me from completing my education.*

For a child to gain full support for his or her education, a triangle must be created between the home, the community, and the school. The parents must stay in close contact with the school, and the community must likewise support the efforts of the school and the parents. This is ideally illustrated when parents from the community are involved in fundraising events, PTA meetings, and field trips with the school. Parents and community members can also volunteer their time with tutoring at the school, or with holiday events that the school sponsors.

The community in which a child grows can either be healthy or unhealthy. The optimal community will be one in which various institutions can operate in tandem to support the child's growth. Thus, a church can be a place not just for worship, but also a place in which a child can find authority figures that can become role models, or even surrogate parents. Families in which the father is absent can benefit greatly from this presence in the community. A minister, priest, or rabbi can guide, counsel, and encourage, and even tutor a young child. The parent, such as a single mother, can find a social support system within the congregation. The church can also augment the values and principles that the child learns at home. This setting can also become a haven of safety in communities where violence is endemic. Another benefit of having close ties to a religious institution is that the child will be exposed to peers whose values will hopefully reflect the values of that institution. Youth groups are common in many community churches of almost any denomination. Many times these youth groups will sponsor outings and field trips. A child from a poor neighborhood might get a chance to visit museums, the beach, or even tour universities. Most colleges and universities are happy to arrange tours for such groups.

In a community one can also find institutions such as libraries that can be of tremendous benefit to a child, especially when the child is already exposed to reading at home. Ideally, the family should take these trips to the library. It should be a shared experience. The important value to promote in this process is an intrinsic love of reading and learning, for its own sake. A current strong debate is whether children should be given "carrots" for reading. The question becomes, should I reward my child for reading a book, or should my child read as part of a lifestyle? There are no easy answers to this question, but parents should realize that as a child enters college, no college professor would offer the young person a new bike for reading a thick college textbook. However, society does provide "carrots" for college graduates in the form of higher salaries and better jobs. But if one uses that argument, one falls prey to the utilitarian view of education as a means merely to a bigger paycheck rather than viewing learning as a way of growing as a person and learning more about oneself along the way. The pastor at my church once gave a sermon about an 87 year-old woman who had finally completed her education as a means of personal growth. She passed away just two months after her commencement ceremony. It had been her lifelong goal and she was no doubt retired by the time that she re-enrolled in college. She was not thinking about a promotion at work, driving a Lexus, a bigger house, or social prestige or status. She merely wanted to learn about the world and the way life works. The privilege of being able to understand the way the world works and one's role in it, and the chance to grow as a human being and become more mature, is worth more than all the "carrots" put together. This is something all groups in our society must realize if they are to gain full benefit and full growth from education.

Museums can also be of incredible benefit to a child's mind. In a museum, a child can gaze upon priceless works of art or see how an automobile functions. From Leonardo da Vinci to bullet trains, the world opens up as a flower to a child in a museum. They can become a haven of learning and refuge from the ugliness of inner cities. They can also augment what they are learning in school. Thus, after attending a "boring" lecture in biology, the child can wander into a science museum and see a "cool" three-dimensional or even virtual reality model of the human brain. Museums have a way of presenting information, much of this textbook information, in a way that is exciting, engaging, colorful, and memorable. Many give discounts to students and cost less than sending a family of four to the movies.

The other haven in a community that can be of benefit to a child is the public park. That's not to say that these places are always safe. It is well known that criminal activity can take place in the light of day in a place such as a park. Thus, one has to be judicious in selecting one that is safe and clean. This can be the site of family picnics, sports events, and municipal swimming. Most cities have a recreation department that arranges sports camps, swimming lessons, crafts, scholastic enrichment programs and other such services to the community. Latinos and other groups who may not feel as safe as they deserve to feel may well find the avenues of growth for their children that they need through their local recreation department.

So far, all of these suggestions have been described in very general terms. What does this mean for the common family on a day-to-day basis? More specifically, what can be done to make sure that a school day is utilized fully? First of all, the ability of a child to get up on time and with the requisite energy for the day is dependent upon the time that the child went to sleep the night before. A very basic tool that parents can implement is a set time every night when the child is expected to bathe, brush his or her teeth, and get into bed. The younger the child, the earlier it should be. For a ten year-old, for instance, 9:00 at night is a reasonable time to expect that child to get ready for bed. For a fifteen year-old, 10:00 is a good time for bed. Ultimately, it is up to the parents' discretion to set the time for homework, dinner, and bedtime, but what is most important is that the parents enforce regularity of these times. Consistency is key. With regularity and consistency, the child will come to internalize the structure and discipline of his or her home life, which they can later use as a tool in either collegiate activities or vocational pursuits as adults. A young child simply needs more sleep and rest than an adult. A child's body produces more energy per hour than even the most energetic of adults. Sleep becomes the main method of recuperating the energy that was expended during the day. Parents need to appreciate the necessary quality of sleep for a child. Sleepiness is one of the main problems that teachers report in their work. Even on a social level, authorities estimate that sleepiness accounts for a high level of traffic and even airplane accidents. Once an adequate night's sleep is attained, the next task is getting up. Parents also have much control over this process in their child's routine. Does the child have an alarm clock or other method of waking the child on time? If not, this would be a worthwhile investment, and alarm clocks are cheaper than ever. Thus, one of the main ways that parents can help their child succeed in school is by organizing their home so that there are rules and set schedules for many activities. As previously mentioned, parents need to establish a set time for a child to go to bed every night. Getting up in the morning must also be a strictly enforced routine. Many children will try to coax their parents into allowing them to watch "just ten more minutes" of television or any other activity that is interfering with bedtime. Parents must assert their authority and enforce the rules calmly. No yelling or theatrics are necessary to enforce the rules calmly and efficiently in the home. The child is thus better able to incorporate the rules rather than develop a desire to rebel against them. Rules that are enforced as calmly as possible are more likely to be internalized by the child rather than becoming something against which the child must rebel.

Natalie Rathvon, Ph.D., in her book *The Unmotivated Child* (1996), gives wonderful suggestions in the way that parents can communicate constructively with their child regarding the child's studies. Often the messages that parents transmit to their child regarding his or her studies are the *unspoken* messages. For instance, many parents try to reward good grades with some sort of material gift or bonus at the end of the school term. However, as Dr. Rathvon points out, what this does is to send a message that

> ". . . learning is not rewarding enough to be engaged in for its own sake; to be rewarding it must be accompanied by material gains. . . . Although parents mean to encourage motivation when they promise to supply external reinforcement such as money or toys for better grades, the message is: "Your school isn't interesting enough to be rewarding in and of itself. We, your parents, know this, so we must give you an external reason to do it." (p. 115–16)

Additionally, as Dr. Rathvon points out, parents that have more than one child and are administering rewards to the child who is not performing satisfactorily, and yet the other child is performing well, pose a conundrum: who gets the prize? If the child performing poorly gets a gift for an improvement in grades, the other child, who has already been diligent in his studies, will feel left out. It sends a double message due to the fact that if good grades are to be rewarded, then the other, high-achieving student should have been receiving rewards all along. She also references several other negative effects of rewards, such as the fact that if parents use rewards, they must usually give bigger and bigger rewards to keep the child motivated over time. She also mentioned the fact that parents who give rewards will inevitably face the time when due to his or her age the giving of rewards must be gradually weaned. The child who was previously rewarded for good grades will usually begin to show deterioration in his or her schoolwork due to the fact that the rewards are no longer being given. However, Dr. Rathvon feels that the most damaging effect of the awarding of gifts for good grades is the fact that the parents who give rewards are sending an unspoken message to the child. As she phrases it,

> "The child who is offered external incentives for good school performance reasons, "Why do my parents need to reward or bribe me to perform? It must be because I am incapable of performing satisfactorily without rewards." Thus rewards for achievement actually strengthen the child's image of himself as inferior and incompetent. Similarly, rewards, especially large rewards, reinforce his belief that his parents value the external product of his performance (grades) more than his internal growth (feelings of competence)." (p. 117–118)

Rathvon, Ph.D. (1996), points to the many ways in which parents can innocently, and unknowingly, exacerbate the problem created when a student is achieving below his or her potential. The many ways in which parents benignly try to encourage their youngster to do better in school may actually further discourage improved performance. Two very common examples she cites are the "You-Can-Do-It Speech," and the "Just-Do-Your-Best Speech." In the first example, the parents try to tell the child that he or she can do better. However, as she states,

> "Unfortunately, when parents tell the child that they know he has the intelligence to do his work, it merely reminds him that he has failed to live up to their expectations. The message that he hears is quite different: "You can do it. So why aren't you doing it?" (p. 143–144)

As she states, the child is likely to connect that speech with feelings of embarrassment and humiliation. Thus, instead of making the child feel better, or encouraged, it makes him or her feel worse. The second speech, as mentioned, is the "Just-Do-Your-Best Speech." Dr. Rathvon (1996), points out how this speech, so commonly given by parents, also has an adverse effect. As she points out, the child already has a view of himself or herself as incompetent. Therefore, the child is likely to translate this speech to one of low parental expectations. As she states,

> ". . . all [the student] hears is that his parents do not expect him to achieve excellence. He hears that they believe he is so incompetent that a mediocre performance is acceptable. With this kind of destructive encouragement, his view of himself as inadequate becomes more entrenched." (p. 144)

As an alternative, she suggests countermeasures to these destructive messages. For instance, Dr. Rathvon (1996) encourages parents to use encouragement in the *here-and-now*. The examples she cites are "You are really working hard on those spelling words," or, "I can see that your are learning to get the hang of word problems," or, "You're really sticking to your study schedule." (p. 145) She references the fact that what is important is that the child be patiently and warmly encouraged to continue the effort. It is the *effort* that must be encouraged. The child must come to associate *effort* with positive results. Internally, the child will gradually begin to achieve these positive results through continued effort.

The other thing that parents must do is to adapt their communication strategies not only to the child's self-esteem, but also they must make an effort to match their expectations of his behavior to the culture of the classroom. Bernhard, et.al. (1997), found that Latin American students in Canada were experiencing similar difficulties as they are in the United States. They reported on a school in which a teacher of a Latin American youngster reported how the student was almost too compliant. They quote the teacher as saying,

"She . . . is too good. The parent have taught her that she has to obey the teacher, that she has to behave well in class, not to interrupt if she does not understand something, she will not put up her hand to ask. In this [Canadian] system if children are not aggressive they stay behind. Many times, she . . . misses an opportunity because she is too slow compared to the others. . . . The parents' efforts to train her in obedience are part of the overall commitment to maintaining her cultural identity." (p. 226)

This points to an inconsistency between the parents' home culture and the culture of the educational system of their host country, in this case, Canada. The critical issue here is the fact that the parents may feel that they are engaging the child, and doing all they must to help him in his education. But, in the end, they are basing their parental techniques on what helped them growing up, in another country and in a different generation. As Bernhard, et.al. (1997), in their study point out, one of the student's parents would spend time with her every night and try to assist her with her homework and checking her report cards, but the parents were still missing the point:

"[The parents] are apparently unaware that the class environment is informally structured and that the teacher calls for a high degree of independence in the children . . . [the student] is not well equipped for the rough-and-tumble interactions which are quite common in her school and classroom as in the Canadian educational system in general. She fails to assert her own views with enough vigor to thrive in the competitive school environment. (p. 226)

There are two forces at play in this scenario. First, the researcher point to the fact that this student's parents were perhaps too concerned with their daughter behaving properly in the classroom. This is a common cultural trait among Latinos. They expect that their children behave obediently in the classroom. This is not entirely a bad cultural tradition. Certainly, the task of both the teacher and the students to cover new material each day will be made a lot easier if the students are compliant. There have been so many stories told by teachers themselves of students misbehaving and, of course, people remember the more horrific incidents involving students who bring guns to school with the express purpose of gunning down their fellow students and teachers. The second force is the linguistic and cultural mismatch between the term *educado*, which merely means compliant and well behaved, in Spanish, with the American-English word *educated*, which means a graduated of a high school, and even college. Latino parents will usually enforce the first, Spanish-language, definition, before they apply the second, English-language definition. Simply put, Latino parents have their priorities out of alignment; they prefer to have well-behaved, quiet little children, rather than have children who are sharp, assertive (with respect to raising their hand to either give an answer or to ask for help) in the classroom, and educationally competitive.

However, in this case, what might, on the surface, seem like a desirable cultural asset, becomes, instead, a cultural liability. As Bernhard, et.al. (1997) point out, "In this situation of cultural mismatch, [the student's] ability to perform is undermined. . . . The more retiring students face a disadvantage . . . its is unfortunately reinforced by [the students] parents' advice to be compliant and obedient. (p. 226–227) The researchers gave another, more promising example, about another young Latino student in the same school. However, in this case, the advantage that this boy had, is that his parents spoke English to him at home. This brings up an extremely important point: this boy's parents placed his academic survival and success above any need, on their part, to keep him bilingual or bicultural. As the researchers stated,

> "[The student's] parents . . . have arrived at their own approach to adaptation in the English-Speaking Canadian setting. Despite their own affirmations of cultural identity in terms of their Latin-American social circle, they are putting their son's survival and success, as they it, above his cultural identity. They are apparently making judgments about the prerequisites for success in Canadian society as they understand it." (p. 230)

The authors conclude that the Canadian teachers' rather negative view of how the Latino parents are preparing, or technically, *not preparing*, their children for success in school has merit. As for the educational system of the United States, it is reasonable to assume that the previous Anglo-Protestant cultural values enumerated by Samuel Huntington (2004), are shared by both the Canadian and American educational systems: academic competitiveness, assertiveness in class, an emphasis on English, and individualism. Thus, the study from Toronto has great relevance to the cultural chasm between Hispanics and Anglo-Americans in the United States.

To conclude, Hispanics must provide not only structure and regularity in their homes, in order to encourage their children to study, but they must also become more familiar with the culture of the school system of the United States. It is a far cry from the classrooms they were familiar with in Mexico, or Nicaragua, or Honduras. Hispanic parents must provide a support system that includes physical, linguistic, intellectual, and material components. All of these are necessary in order to raise educationally prepared children in the United States.

Chapter Seven

Educating the Uneducable

As has been previously shown, the number of Hispanics who do not complete their high school education is considerable. Hispanics also have a long tradition of not complete a college education. This has its roots in the Latino culture itself, which is characteristically low in self-discipline and drive. It almost comes to create the impression, however superficially, that Hispanics are *uneducable*. I know for a fact that this is not true. Otherwise, I would not have gone through such lengths as to write this treatise on the possible improvements that must be made in the Hispanic community. I do believe that Hispanics are capable of becoming educated. The very fact that they have been graduating from college has been a positive sign of growth in that area. All that needs to be done now is to increase the numbers doing so. Additionally, serious changes in the Latino culture are needed if Hispanics are to reach educational parity with other groups. One of the ways in which they can achieve this parity is to begin merely completing their high school and college graduation rates. These high school and college graduates can then go on to become mentors for students still in high school. If not mentoring, then some other measures must be implemented. As Victor Davis Hanson references in his book, *Mexifornia* (2003),

> ". . . just reaching the remedial [California State University] programs is a great achievement in itself [for Latinos]. Despite millions in federal and state expenditures in the last twenty years, by 1996 only 61 percent of Hispanics?both native and foreign-born?had graduated from high school. Nearly a decade later, out of every 100 Hispanics?native or foreign born, illegal or lawful immigrants, citizens or aliens?who now enter California high schools, *30 will drop out*. And of the remaining 70, fewer than 4 will matriculate prepared for any serious college-level courses in mathematics. Less than 10 percent of all adult Mexican-Americans currently *hold a bachelor's degree*." (p. 123–124)

Thus, what has to happen first is that Hispanics must be equipped with the ability to graduate from high school. Which begs the question: Why do they drop out of high school? There are several reasons why students in general, and Hispanic students in particular, will ultimately drop out of high school. The reasons, among others, have to do with: communication, educational advantage, psychological adjustment to school culture, family finances, teen pregnancy, and gang-, or peer-related influences.

Among the reasons, one must first list a breakdown in communication. For a student to drop out of high school, there will already have been many warning sign which were either ignored, unnoticed, or somehow were unheeded. The act of dropping out of high school should not, in the end, be viewed as the ultimate problem, but rather the inevitable end result of many things that went wrong further back in a student's education. When referencing a breakdown in communication, one refers mainly to communication along three channels: (1) communication between parents and the teacher(s), (2) communication between parents and their child, and (3), between the child and the teacher(s). It is a challenge to find a hierarchy to determine which of these three lines of communication is the most important. Therefore, in order to make the point most clearly, we will assume, for the moment, that all three lines of communication are equally important.

The first line of communication, between parents and the teacher, must be kept open and perpetually active in order for parents to be apprised of any downturn in their child's academic performance. As previously mentioned, if parents do not speak, read, or write English, it will be difficult for them to remain informed of their child's progress in school. This is why the recommendation was made earlier for a bilingual staff at the school so that every effort can be made to reach the parents and to communicate to them the developments in their child's education. Teachers, as mentioned, also must make every effort to be in frequent contact with the parents, even if a translator is necessary. A strong case can be made, of course, for the necessity of having all migrant parents learn English so as to facilitate this process of communication in the schools. Here, however, we will focus mainly on the practicality of the situation as it is currently with regard to Hispanic parents' limited English ability. PTSA meetings may not be enough for parents to be regularly reminded, or kept abreast of, how well their child is doing is school. Parents should be encouraged to make regular contact with the child's teacher in order to understand the difficulties, if any, that their child may be having with the school material.

In high school, once an adolescent reaches an older age, the natural progression will dictate that the adolescent take greater responsibility for his or her education. This will necessitate an open line of communication between the adolescent and his teachers. However, in the early grades, such as grades one through eight, it will fall on the parents to make sure that they are kept well informed of any new developments, both positive and negative.

The second line of communication involves parents and their children. This will involve such routine habits as checking in each and every day with their child to see how their day at school went, and what feelings they had about different events at school. Parents should remain more or less vigilant for early warning signs that things may not be proceeding smoothly. It does not take an advanced degree in psychology to understand the warning signs that a student may be having, or experiencing, academic or psychological difficulties. At an early age, both psychological and academic problems will compound each other, and their mutual impact can be particularly worrisome. Withdrawal, a laconic attitude, and rebelliousness are all clear signals that a student is beginning to display psychological problems involving his social, personal, and academic adjust, which may need remediation. Otherwise, if left unaddressed, these will impact the youngster's academic progress upstream.

As mentioned above, dropping out of school does not occur in a vacuum. Many earlier warning signs that were left unheeded will usually precede it. Parents must sit down every day with their child, perhaps after school, or at the dinner table, and ask them directly, "How was your day at school?" or, "How did you *feel* at school today?" Parents must enter the inner psychological world of their child in order to understand the answers to such a question. Parents can come to understand the meaning of their child's responses by coming to understand the impressions that each day will bring to a young child's senses. They can be made aware that a child's level of communication will not be the same as an adult. For instance, in response to the previous two questions, one will not typically get a thirteen-year-old to say much more than "fine." This is why parents must ask open-ended questions that are inviting, rather than closed-ended questions that yield only a "yes," or "no" response. Thus, parents should avoid asking, "Did you enjoy your day at school?" or, "Was everything O.K. at school today?" Obviously, a child will typically answer such questions with a one-word response, and will march off to his or her room, close the door, and not be seen until dinner. *End of discussion*.

Natalie Rathvon, Ph.D., in her book *The Unmotivated Child* (1996), suggests that parents ask questions that have a psychologically inviting nature:

"What was the field trip to the museum like?"
"How can your mother and I help you with your essay?"
"Could you tell me about your ideas for your science project?"
    . . . By inviting rather than demanding communication, the open question demonstrates that parents are interested in what the child is doing and how he's

feeling, but does so without criticizing or interrogating the child. Paradoxically, because it is the least demanding type of question, it is more likely than any other to get a meaningful answer." (p. 140–141)

Furthermore, she recommends that parents begin to understand the reason that adolescents make use of absolutes in their communication. As she explains, the use of absolutes is intended to communicate a youngster's anxieties about his performance in class. These absolutes may not have the face value of meaningful communication, but nevertheless are intended to communicate a feeling of worry. Many parents do not pick up on these subtle hints that adolescents use in their speech. This is why it is so crucial that parents begin to get *behind* the usage of very negative or "juvenile" language, which most adolescents use. Such language and phrasing, as "I'll never get this!" or, "This class is *boring*," or, "Who *needs* this class?" are only intended to communicate anxiety and a sense of incompetence. Parents typically respond to such statements in a way that is rather unsympathetic, such as: "Gee, that's too bad," or, "I'm sorry to hear that," or, "Well, that's life!" Answers such as those merely sweep the problem under the proverbial carpet and leave the problem unaddressed. Instead, parents should respond to such statements in a manner that further invites the adolescent to communicate his troubles, such as: "*Why* do you feel you'll never understand it?" or, "*What* makes your class so boring?" or, "*Why* do you feel you don't need this class?" Parents must listen with a *third ear* in order to understand what their adolescent is trying to convey. Only then can parents approach their youngster with the intent of getting him or her to open up more, psychologically (and verbally!) about school. The parents can then encourage the youngster to come up with the solution to the problem.

The third level of communication is that between the student and the teacher. Instructors must not only convey warmth and understand to the student who is having trouble, but must also make time available if a student needs more time with him or her. Of course, the communication skills that students bring with them into the classroom are usually a reflection of the way they were raised. This once again throws the responsibility back onto the parents to raise their children with effective communication skills. This also relates to Attachment Theory as described earlier, in which a child who has developed a *secure attachment* to authority figures, beginning with his parents, will come to view them as helpful and available. Of course, there is every possibility that the teacher may be unhelpful and unavailable. There are such teachers. In this case, which is entirely possible, a student must demonstrate and utilize his ability to communicate with an unhelpful or unavailable teacher. If a child is able to communicate his needs effectively to a teacher then the appropriate remedy can be discovered between them, collaboratively, such as staying after school, finding supplemental tutoring, extra material, or even an outside source, such as the Sylvan Learning Centers. It is entirely possible that a student may misinterpret the harried and busy schedule of the teacher as evidence that the teacher *does not care*. In her book, *Issues In Latino Education* (2003) Mariella Espinoza-Herold quoted a Latina student she interviewed who complained that "Some teachers are too busy lecturing, talking to themselves at a different level, not at our level." (p. 78) Many adolescents, due to their developmental stage, will misinterpret teachers' behavior as implying disinterest. This is why the communication barrier must be broken so that a child can communicate his needs to the teacher.

There are other reasons for the problem of students dropping out of high school. According to Mariella Espinoza-Herold (2003), "A common perception among public school educators and the public in general is that minority students drop out of school because of personal deficiencies, language difficulties, poverty, and many other perceived culturally ingrained pathologies." (p. 117) More problematically, is the phenomenon that many Latino students find themselves in opposition to school authorities. This betrays a certain failure within the culture to inculcate the meaning of the term, *educado*, which, as mentioned previously, refers to being respectful of authority figures, and being well behaved. Latino parents often criticize Anglo children for being mouthy with their parents, yet Latino students are quite unruly in school. Mariella Espinoza-Herold found that the students she interviewed had consistent run-ins with school authorities and were oppositional to the rules and discipline that are *de rigueur* of the school culture. There seems to be distrust on the part of many Latino students to the authorities in school, perceiving them to be insensitive. As Mariella Espinoza-Herold stated,

> "[The students interviewed] in this study consistently voiced their opinions not only on the lack of connection between their life experiences and the school curricula but also on their negative interactions with school authorities and teachers, the school policies, the teacher and administrative insensitivity to students' emerging adult roles, and the lack of respect for their language and [cultural] identity." (p. 117)

Although it might be very tempting for social researchers to empathize with the students' perception of the school authorities as cruel and insensitive, or even racist, one must be very critical in evaluating this position. To look at a high school and examine the Hispanic dropouts and listen to their grievances overlooks the facts that other, non-Hispanic students from the same high school are successfully graduating and going on to college. If we are listening only to the reports of the Hispanic students, without further investigating the problem, we would be making a mistake in believing every word they say and placing the blame for the students' problems on the teachers and administrators.

One must remember that these are, in the end, adolescents. Teens are normally hormonal, and boys especially are likely to have upheavals of testosterone that may cause them to become more belligerent and bellicose in defiance of their teachers. Teenagers are by their very nature, very emotional and prone to passions that may cause them to make attributions in their search for causes in other people's behavior. Their thinking is very much emotion-based. For instance, if a teacher is walking past a student, and says, "I'm sorry, Ramone, I need to get to a meeting right now," Ramone might, due to his teenage mentality, interpret his teacher's words as a reflection that *the teacher does not care*. If, however, Ramone were to approach the teacher the next day, and tell him or her, calmly and politely, that he needs help with trigonometry, the teacher might then give him his full attention, and find a way to get Ramone the help he needs. *Thus, the psychological reasons that students explain for their decision to drop out of high school, such as a sense of alienation, abandonment, or even a ethnic clash between their culture and the culture of the school may be based, in part, on their emotionally misguided attributions, which have a want of logic.* There are, no doubt, many adolescents who will most likely feel a very real sense of abandonment and alienation. These are the students that perhaps come from a single parent home, and that parent works all day. This includes latchkey children and adolescents. It is crucial that teachers working with this population of students understand the lack of support systems in the students' lives in order to comprehend why a student may be having academic or emotional difficulty, and may be on the cusp of dropping out. As with any relationship, a teacher-student relationship requires a mutuality of effort and communication, as well as mutual understanding. Teachers must understand that Latinos, by and large, come from poor neighborhoods. By understanding the lack of resources in the lives of Hispanic adolescents, they may be able to brainstorm with their students on creative ways to find solutions to the students' difficulties. One of the ways, as previously mentioned, is a system of mentoring for Latino students. This would entail matching a Latino elementary school student with a high school freshman. Latino high school freshmen would be paired with Latino high school graduates, preferably now enrolled in college. Preferably, the same mentor would mentor the student for the entire four years of high school. There could even be mentors for Latino college freshmen, especially those Latinos who are working and taking a smattering of courses at a local community college. Research shows that this population of Latino community college students is usually the most at-risk of permanently dropping out of college. The reason this would be a great benefit for Latino students is that the Latino parents themselves may not be high school or college graduates, and may not understand what is necessary to traverse the high school curriculum and excel in certain courses, such as AP, or Advanced Placement classes, and score highly on the SAT, or the ACT.

On another level, what has to take place in order for Latinos to make themselves more "educable" is for them to abandon the poisonous Chicano Studies departments in the universities, both public and private. Since the late cultural revolution of the last quarter of the twentieth century, these departments have done more to poison the minds of Latino college students and have done little to truly advance their educational success in the United States. As Hanson (2003) states,

"The catalog of courses of any California university reveals the intellectual world that immigrants and their children can be press-ganged into. . . . Introduction to Chicano Spanish; Methodology of the Oppressed; Barrio Popular Culture; Body, Culture and Power; Chicana Feminism; History of the Chicano; History of the Chicano Movement; History of the Chicano and Chicana Worker; Racism in American History; Chicano Political Organizing; Chicano Writers; De-Colonizing Cyber-Cinema; Dance of the Chicano; and dozens more. The history department offerings included thirteen similar courses on Latino and Chicano issues, in addition to more generic classes on race and oppression. But the entire catalog had only one class on the Civil War per se, "Civil War and Reconstruction." There were no real courses dedicated to the Revolutionary War or World War II." (p. 105)

The only thing these college departments have done is to further alienate Latino college students from the mainstream Anglo-Protestant culture, and to perpetuate a culture schism between Hispanics and Anglo-Americans and between Hispanic culture and Anglo-Protestant culture in the United States. As Hanson (2003) states, ". . . if America were so discriminatory and racist, and Mexico for its part such a wonderful society, why would any Mexican . . . come north to such a certified hell-hole?" (p. 107)

By allowing these college courses to thrive, university officials have turned a blind eye to the deconstructive nature of having such blatantly *reverse racist* college courses offered at these universities. In order to begin educating the "uneducable," we must begin to reorient the way that the educational curriculum is structured. *It is high time that American higher education return to the curriculum of yore that emphasized the basics of American history, American culture, American political systems, and America's relation to the world.* These Chicano Studies courses add very little to a college student's moral or intellectual development while matriculating through a university. As Hanson (2003) states,

"Does anyone doubt that a resident alien from Mexico in her first year of college, should she enroll in Latin, classical studies and European history courses, might gain more knowledge of America's heritage and learn the basics of grammar and syntax in ways impossible in "Chicano Body, Culture, and Power"? Or better yet, would not a classics major of Mexican heritage gain more self-esteem through real achievement and mastery of literature than by picking up clichés and slogans from the 1960s recycled in today's "postcolonial" history classes?" (p. 107)

Furthermore, he states, "So far, not one study has shown how a La Raza studies department has affected the tragedy that between 30 and 40 percent of all Hispanics won't graduate from high school." (p. 108) Recently, I was listening to the radio, and I heard a disc jockey ask a caller in a radio contest "Who was the first American president?" The answer a caller gave? Abraham Lincoln. Of course, most Americans can tell you that the correct answer is George Washington. What we are currently witnessing in the United States is a gradual breakdown in real education. One educational curriculum for all Americans that teaches the basics that were taught generations ago. Latinos have not only segregated themselves into their Chicano Studies departments at the universities, but they furthermore feel the need to isolate and segregate themselves with separate college graduation ceremonies. I was invited to the Latino student's graduation ceremony at the University of La Verne, and I declined to attend. I believe that it is damaging for our society to have such movements such as separate college graduation ceremonies held only for Latino students. It further alienates the races from each other. This is another example of reverse racism in that these Latino student graduation ceremonies presumably no Caucasian college graduates would be allowed to participate. How would the Latino students feel if the Caucasian students held a whites-only graduation ceremony in which no Latino graduates would be allowed to attend? I am certain that the Latino student populations on any college campus would march straight to the office of the president in order to seek redress of this grievance. The Latino students would see a whites-only graduation ceremony as racist, yet that is the very thing Latino students are doing by having these exclusive ceremonies on Commencement Day. This is culturally chauvinistic, reverse racist, and self-isolating on the part of the Latino students. In a very real sense, the cultural isolation that Hispanics are prone to lament is the very isolation they have created with their self-isolating behavior, self-segregating ceremonies, and self-isolating use of the Spanish language. If we are to educate Hispanics, or better yet, if Hispanics are to educate themselves, they must adopt English, communicate respectfully to their teachers any personal difficulties they might be having, abandon the Chicano Studies departments in college, and join the rest of the non-Hispanic students in celebrating their college graduation ceremonies. Any social movement which is a "just-for-us" movement, will tend to isolate that group from everyone else and cause any alienation from other groups in society, no matter how benign its goal or intent. Once Latinos join the work force, they cannot self-isolate themselves anymore. They will be forced (in a way, privileged) to work and interact with African Americans, Asians, Middle-Easterners, and Europeans, as well as Caucasians. The movement seen in the universities will only train Hispanics to isolate themselves in a society that is increasingly the adoptive home to people of many cultures and ethnicities, not just Latinos. Thus, if we are to raise a new generation of future employees, and citizens who can effectively engage and appreciate people of other non-Hispanic cultures, this self-isolating movement seen in the universities must end. Only then will we begin to see the real education of Hispanics begin to emerge.

A true college education affords people more life choices. It definitely affords greater vocational choices as well as vocational flexibility. Latinos must find ways to avail themselves of all the advantages that a college education can bring. Aghop Der-Karabetian, Ph.D., from the University of La Verne, once informed me that the concept of a liberal arts education has lost hold in modern society as more and more people begin to focus on the "practical" aspects of education. It appears more and more young people want to understand why they need to know the Pythagorean theorem if they will never use it when they work as, say, a journalist. What many young people fail to understand, he informed me, is that the smattering of courses that one receives in a liberal arts education allows one to develop critical thinking skills, which can be introduced into almost any workplace environment. The design of a liberal arts curriculum should not be seen as a waste of time. Rather, it should be seen as an opportunity to flex one's mental muscles as one delves into the areas of history, math, political science, literature, and so on. This helps to make the mind adaptable. *College is intended to make one a free thinker.*

Vocational education, on the other hand, is rather specialized in focus. The realities in the lives of many Hispanics make trade schools a viable and practical option. As a graduate of a vocational school, I can attest to the useful nature of such schools for those whose lifestyles cannot accommodate a university education. However, there is a definite disadvantage of attending a trade school. The technological nature of our society is constantly at the mercy of the rapidly changing nature of computer systems. The computer programs and software on which one trains at a vocational school may be replaced entirely within a few years. This renders the student of a vocational school somewhat dependent on that school to continually train him or her on the newer and more sophisticated systems. On a very real level, lifelong education should be a goal for people. Even as one who possesses a master's degree, I have found the need to continue my schooling at various institutions. However, in my case, it is a matter more of refinement than replacement. Replacement is exactly what will take place if one learns a specialized trade involving technology that may change or be outmoded within a few years. The trade schools, while a necessary asset in society, may, in the long run, keep Latinos still behind those with college degrees. What accounts for such a high enrollment of Latinos in the trade schools? On a very basic level, these may very well be students whose academic skills were never properly honed in their elementary and high school education. The Latino population may very well have placed itself into the trade schools as a result of a cultural tradition of focusing more on practicality rather than a view of education that would have been more in line with Jefferson's conception of a university education during the Enlightenment in which he lived.

For any cultural group who has faced privation, hunger, political turmoil, and personal tragedies over many generations, the matter of mere survival will become one's main goal in life. How can one focus on the stylistic differences of writers in the Romantic period when one has six children to feed, ailing parents, and difficulty finding work? Over centuries, any group can fall victim to the need to focus on what is salient, what is real, what is happening here and now. Any group can end up needing to focus on very basic needs for survival. When Hispanics immigrate to the United States, they bring with them this need to focus on *practical* realities. They will need work, they will need shelter, and they will need to feed their young. They will also need to learn English. They start the race already behind by mere virtue of the fact that their subsistence needs may not be satisfactorily met. This points to a clash of cultures. One culture, Anglo-Protestant culture, already has its established institutions and support systems in place. Hispanics, on the other hand, may have trouble even meeting basic needs. But what may not be occurring is the recognition among the more beleaguered groups that in order to rise in society, one must attain a university degree. Chip Anderson, Ph.D., from Azusa Pacific University, mentioned a statistic that I found startling. If one invests $50,000 on a university degree, the ultimate rate of return by way of increased earnings is $700,000 over a lifetime. So a person with a college degree earns, on average, almost three quarters of a million dollars more over a lifetime than one that does not possess a college degree. And the figures may be higher for certain industries.

Another benefit of a college education is the personal growth that occurs within the mind of the student. One rarely graduates from college being the same person as when one first enrolls. One learns greatly about oneself, one's background, one's place in the world, and one's gifts. This ties in with what Aghop Der-Karabetian, Ph.D., from the University of La Verne told me about the value of a liberal arts education. It produces an informed citizenry. An educated citizenry will ultimately be better equipped to handle emergencies on a local, state, and even national level. The events of September 11, 2001 are a vivid reminder that America needs an educated citizenry capable of thinking through situations involving terrorist threats and international turmoil. As the events in the Middle East become more complex, the United States will need future generations of college graduates that can safely navigate this country through the choppy political waters in which we now find ourselves.

Another answer to the question of "why education?" can be understood in the concept of contribution. As one progresses through college, one can better understand how one's talents can be used for the greater good of society. It might be incorrect to assume that service is a uniquely American concept, but it is a strong national virtue. A liberal arts education will give a student the chance to understand the injustices of the world and the problems that perpetuate these injustices. From a famine in Africa or a plague in India, or the deforestation of Brazil, the student gains a view of the world in which the problems of this world are brought forth more vividly and ultimately understood more completely than ever before. This is linked to the process of learning a set of values and principles. A university education can, theoretically, contribute a set of moral guidelines that can serve as a complement to the ones that one learns at home. Many universities promote the virtues that they try to inculcate in the student body. Almost all universities have touted all service, humility, community, and contribution, as part of their ethos. Thus, the benefit of an education is not to be measured purely by raw textbook knowledge. This is a glaring misperception in many people about the end results of getting a college degree. This is why people are rarely the same after they graduate from college. There is a very subtle development of humility within the student that will present itself more clearly in the sense of mission at graduation. They are no longer thinking about themselves at that point, but rather their role in giving back to the world their gifts that were inculcated at the university.

This collegiate sense of mission and purpose is what will ultimately allow our world to overcome the plagues of modern society: ecological degradation, violence, drug addiction, alcoholism, and diseases. It takes an educated citizenry, with sufficient wisdom, to overcome, or at least come close to overcoming, these modern problems. Every day, medical students at various research universities are busily attempting to understand the genetic and dietetic underpinnings of heart disease, cancer, diabetes, and a host of other diseases in the hopes of permanently ridding them from society. Likewise, social scientists, such as university psychologists, are trying to understand how to better treat various psychological disorders in the hopes of bringing emotional alleviation to those beset by such conditions. It can become an exciting enterprise to join the ranks of such individuals and become a part of the team that specializes in a problem, chipping away at it little by little each day. These diverse professions can become the most rewarding and meaningful in modern society. I am confident that Latinos have in them the talents and gifts that can be put to service in these professions. There are already sizeable numbers of Hispanics in medicine, law, finance, and psychology as well as many other professional fields. My own mission, then, becomes one of increasing the numbers of Hispanics in these professions. That is my enduring inheritance from my university education.

The real cultural value of a college degree is that it broadens one's horizons; it enlarges one's understanding of oneself and one's world, and gives one vocational flexibility. There is, however, another social aspect to having a college degree. Our society has an 800-year lead on the Middle Ages. There is still a very subtle, almost imperceptible, hierarchy that has been handed down from medieval Europe between those who have a degree and those who do not. Like it or not, this social ladder is intact, and it is still felt that those with a college degree are socially superior. This is truly unfortunate. No one is superior to anyone else because of a diploma. Human value cannot be measured in such terms. Even those without a degree may have very special gifts that need to be fostered regardless of whether that person ever attains a degree or not. One of my personal heroes, Charles Lindbergh, flunked out of the University of Wisconsin at Madison. He went on to become not only a great flyer and test pilot, but also a great orator when he became head of the America First movement, a political group that opposed American intervention in the aggression begun by the Nazis in Europe. His speeches on American isolationism have been some of the most eloquent I have ever read. Thus, he serves as proof that one does not need a college degree to become a highly effective person in society. But, the true benefit of a college degree lies in bringing out the hidden talents and aptitudes that had always been a part of one's God-given nature. Going to college allows the seeds and buds of hidden talents to be nurtured and brought to full blossom.

Chapter Eight

College—"The Final Frontier"

To Boldly Go Where No Family Member Has Gone Before

The decision to send a student to college must be made when the child is still in elementary school, and it must be firm, thereby becoming an inevitable future event in the child's mind. It must be made explicitly clear to the child that the world will open up to him or her while in college. The idea has to be planted with positive affirmation and optimistic faith in the child's ability to reach college on his or her own merit. What has to be emphasized is how much fun and exciting, as well as challenging, college can be.

There is a notion, common among many people, that college is merely a place where one attends lectures and reads textbooks. The implicit idea in this notion is that what one walks away with after graduating from college is merely the accumulation of facts and tidbits of useless information with no connection to the "real world." Among Latinos in particular, especially those from lower socioeconomic levels, there will be fierce focus on *utility*. What they must realize is that the university experience is so much more than mere intellectual minutiae. One gains an expansion of self-awareness, growth, and social consciousness not otherwise attainable from the "real world." Additionally, many Latino parents will view the bachelor's degree as the ticket to a profession. This may not necessary be the case. A liberal arts degree is merely an *introduction* to a field of study. However, the growth that occurs in the four years during which the degree is earned is worth more than any specific job skill that could otherwise be gained in career training.

Latinos, as has been made very clear throughout this book, have made gains, but have a further distance to travel to attain parity with other groups when it comes to a college education. According to Leonard A. Valverde, in *The Latino Student's Guide to College Success* (2002),

> "In 1999 the Educational Testing Service (ETS) reported that only 22 percent [of Latinos] were enrolled in college. Of this small number, between 60 and 80 percent are enrolled in two-year technical or community colleges. And the statistics get worse: of the low percentage of Latinos admitted to college, only about 5 to 10 percent graduate with a four-year college degree. Again, in 1999 ETS reported that only 8.9 percent of this population group completed four years of college. Few go on to graduate education for a terminal and/or professional degree (4 to 5%), and only about 2 to 3 percent successfully finish their program of study." (p. x)

Once the decision has been reached to go to college, there are several questions that must be answered. Will one choose a public or a private university? The primary difference between a public and a private university lies in the fact that a public university receives its funding from the state. In California, there is a three-tiered system of public colleges. First, there are the California community colleges. There are currently 107 such colleges in the state. Community colleges offer a 2-year degree. This can either be an Associate of Arts, or an Associate of Science degree. Both require roughly sixty units to complete. If a student attends a community college full-time, and also takes classes during the summer term, the 2-year degree can be completed in what will become the freshman and sophomore years of college. If a student decides to only pursue a 2-year degree, then one should not view it necessarily as freshman and sophomore work. It is a 2-year degree, simply that. One also has the option of earning a vocational certificate. These require fewer than the sixty units required for an associate degree. The vocational certificates are offered for certain trades. The Associate of Arts degrees usually have concentrations in one of the liberal arts. Many students, however, opt to transfer to a 4-year college or university after they have completed the necessary prerequisites for such a transfer. The benefit of the community college is primarily financial. The fees are much lower than what would be charged for tuition at a 4-year college or university.

The second tier is comprised of the University of California system. There are nine campuses in California. At the University of California, students can earn a Bachelor of Arts or a Bachelor of Science degree. Students can then go on to earn a master's degree. The UC schools also offer doctorate degrees. This is due to the fact that the schools in the University of California system are research-based. It is usually the case that an institution that has research facilities will be the one to award a doctorate degree. Some schools in the University of California system have gained world class status, such as

UCLA and UC Berkeley. The third tier in this system is comprised of the California State University System. There are 23 campuses in this system. These universities offer Bachelor of Arts and Bachelor of Science degrees. They also offer master's degrees. These schools, however, are not research-based, thus they do not offer doctorates. An additional category that deserves attention is comprised of private universities. As privately funded institutions, these schools are free to establish their own guidelines and criteria as well as the type of degree conferred. There are some world-renowned private universities in California, the most notable being the University of Southern California and Stanford. In the United States, the most famous universities are private schools. Harvard, Yale, Princeton, Brown, Dartmouth, Notre Dame, Radcliffe, and Bryn Mawr are all private institutions. By their very nature, each is very competitive and the selection criteria are very stringent.

Each university will set its own admission criteria. In California, for instance, students need a very high grade point average to gain entry into the State University and the University of California systems. Private schools in California vary in their selection criteria. Some require higher SAT or ACT scores than others. One must investigate what entrance requirements have to be met and by when.

Once a student has decided to go to college, the next step is to select the college or university that best fits the needs of the aspiring young scholar. Many questions will need to be addressed. For instance, can the student go out-of-state, or even out of the country, as an exchange student? Some students are very independent and look forward to being on the opposite side of the country and in a new environment as they attend a university. Other students want to stay in their home state, but will want to go to the other end of the state. This approximates being in a new land. For many Latinos, family obligations may keep them close to home. If this cannot be helped, then there are still many options open to potential Latino college students. Each state in the United States has options for youth to go to college. Even the most dismal of circumstances should not deter Latino youth from applying to college.

Next is the stage at which applicants contact the college to which they want to apply. With the popularity and appeal of the Internet, there are now high quality Web pages for practically every college and university in the country. These Web pages are interactive, colorful, and will most likely contain all the information an applicant may want to know about a college or university. In addition, one can find information about the different departments and faculty. The cost of tuition and registration fees may also be posted on the Web site. Many of these sites might also contain the application for admission. Part of the process of deciding on a college or university may entail visiting different colleges and universities in person. This has been referred to as "college shopping." Only by setting foot on a campus can one ascertain whether a particular school will be a good fit for oneself. There has to be a synergy between the energies one brings to a college campus and the school itself. Some schools are very artsy, some very liberal. Some universities are politically conservative, others very liberal. Each college campus will have its own culture. Latino parents should be actively involved in the process of getting to know the culture of the college to which their son or daughter is applying. This is not to say that parents should be too controlling at this stage of their son or daughter's development. By the time a youngster enrolls in a university, they are usually eighteen. That is the legal age of adulthood. It is important that the young person begin to learn the lessons of responsibility while in college, even if there are a few "hard lessons" along the way. Nevertheless, Hispanic parents need to stay abreast of the college environment in which their son or daughter will be immersed. For instance, many of the public colleges and universities have a high drinking rate on campus. Alcohol has become equated with college life. The connection between college study and drinking dates back to the Middle Ages. Nevertheless, Latino parents should know that their son or daughter will be drinking while in college. One must be twenty-one years old to drink. That may mean illegal and clandestine drinking in the dorms. I am not, even for a second, advocating this. My role in describing this reality to Latino parents is to alert them to the realities of college life. The reality of drinking on campus has been parodied extensively. One movie that attempted to show this as humorously as possible was *National Lampoon's Animal House*. More recently, Aaron Karo wrote a book titled *Ruminations On College Life* (2002). In it, he described the tipsy life of a college student:

> In this new century I think there is going to be a greater effort by colleges to cut down on the amount of drinking done by their students. I also think these attempts will fail miserably. This is because administrators think that kids drink because there is nothing else to do. . . . The problem is, kids don't drink because there's nothing else to do; they drink because they like getting bombed! If anything, we need more *drinking* options. If schools want to cut down on their students' consumption of alcohol, they should try coming up with something else that makes you forget all your worries and makes ugly [people] look good! (p. 109)

The culture of the university will leave an indelible impression upon the student, especially if the student stays the full four years. This is also going be a chance for a young person to make new friends and socialize as never before. A wonderful aspect of college is that young people come together in a common goal, or enterprise, of becoming scholars. It creates a common bond; everyone there is enrolled and studying in a major. Everyone there will hopefully graduate. Everyone roots for the same team during college football games. Yet, in the end, the major benefit of going to college is that young people get the chance to discover who they really are. Much of this realization comes about through all of the socializing in which one engages. One gets to meet people from all walks of life. There are students from every ethnic and cultural group. There are students from every conceivable religious background. Socioeconomic backgrounds will also be quite varied, depending on the university.

Another aspect, which prospective students will have to figure out before they go to college, is whether they will live on or off campus. For many students, life in a dorm can be an interesting, if somewhat crowded existence. As Aaron Karo wrote:

> "College kids live in what amounts to a glorified closet. We have put our beds on cinderblocks just to have room for our clothes. Prisoners don't even have to do that! . . . No matter how small your dorm room is, though, it is where you will have some of your best college moments. It's where you will pre-game with your best friends. It's where you will boot when you've had one tequila shot too many. It's where you will fight with your roommate about his terrible taste in music. And it is where you will hook up with the girl down the hall and then try to avoid seeing her for the rest of the semester. And by the time you move out of the dorm, you'll realize, for a tiny room, you really got a lot of use out of it." (p. 15–16)

On a very real level, living in a dorm will be very different from living at home. The student will have very little privacy as he or she is always paired with a roommate. One may have to put up with distracting music, telephone calls, a messy bathroom, and so on, from a college dorm roommate. Yet, many a college students were enduring those things at home with his siblings. The space will be small, though. And of course there is the issue of a lack of privacy if one wants to bring home a date and enjoy sexual intimacy. There will usually be an RA, or Residential Advisor, who will basically act as warden and landlord for the residence halls.

Once a student has decided to go to college, he or she will need letters of recommendation. This will have to be obtained while still in high school. The student should take care to read the application packet carefully to see what it is that the college is looking for in the letter of recommendation. The student must also read carefully to note when the letter is due. The College Board has written helpful recommendations for students and their parents regarding all aspects of applying to college. With regard to the letters of recommendation, the Board suggests that high school students approach their English or math teachers for letters of recommendation. The teacher or staff member of the high school should at least be someone in a key position to recognize the strengths that the student will bring to college. The Board recommends that the child have a resume at the ready. This will help the recommendation writer. No doubt many teachers and counselors will be besieged with requests for letters of recommendations to colleges from seniors getting ready to complete their final year of high school. A resume will help jog the memory of the person who will write the letter. In addition, they recommend that the student waive the right to view the recommendation letters on the college application itself. The student should also follow up with the recommendation after a few weeks have passed, to ensure that they are being written on schedule. After the letter of recommendation has been written, The College Board recommends that the applicant write a thank you note. I agree. The applicant never knows when he or she will need another favor from the person who wrote the letter.

Another reality about the college social scene is sex. Yes, sex. My own variation on the cliché about the birds and the bees is: birds do it, bees do it, and even busy college students do it. The average college student will go through a few lovers while in college. This is not applicable to all students. Certainly this may not be the case in the private religious schools, but the reality of sex on campus is not to be denied. College becomes a social scene and the laws of attraction are as vivid and alive on college campuses as they are in high school. What makes college different from high school is the fact that the students are no longer under their parents' domain. They now can make their own rules and are accountable to no one. Well, perhaps they are accountable to the Residential Advisor. The ease of availability of contraception and the fact that the off-campus students are no longer living at home increases the likelihood of sex taking place on campus. One way that students hook up is to find someone at a frat party, which brings me to the next section.

The fraternity and sorority houses and groups are another aspect of college campus culture. A fraternity is a collegiate social service club for men. A sorority is the same, for women. There is a specific day called Rush during the early part of the academic year. All the houses will attempt to recruit new members. New members will go to the house that is being leased, or owned, by the specific fraternity or sorority that they want to join. There is normally a very secret initiation pledge activity. The old joke is that it usually involves swallowing live goldfish with beer. I am sure that the pledges are more varied than that. Nevertheless, these initiation activities are very secret and once the applicant has officially pledged himself or herself to a particular house, it's official. He's in. She's in. The membership is for life. Like the Mafia! The fraternities and sororities all have Greek letters, so it is not uncommon to hear of houses of Gamma Phi Kappa, or Delta Gamma Kappa. Many of them will have a strong social service component. Their own self-promotion may high-light their social service as their long-standing tradition. Nevertheless, the parties they throw are formidable. As Karo (2002) wrote: "Being part of the Greek system means going to a lot of mixers, date parties, semiformals, and formals—all names dreamt up by sorority chicks." (p. 57) All kidding aside, this can become a place to meet new people and develop lifelong friendships. Of course, not every student was meant to pledge to a fraternity or sorority. Those who are not, referred to as Independents, are normally just as enriched by their college experiences as those in the Greek clubs. I was an Independent. When I entered Long Beach State University, I was completely ab-sorbed in my studies. I was once invited to a fraternity house party. I remember going out to the backyard, to escape the blaring music, and found many beer cans floating in the pool. A girl later approached me, put her arms around me, gave me a hug, and told me that I was "so awesome." Now, I may be an awesome dude, but this girl didn't know who I was. I was a complete stranger, and she was obviously drunk. I don't normally drink to the point of inebriation. That just is not something I find amusing or fun. To me, this girl's flattering comment about my being awesome, true as that may be, didn't have any merit because of her drunkenness. However, I took it in stride, stayed awhile, and went home. I laugh about it now. There will be those who thrive in that environment, and those are precisely the students that should join. It is not for everyone. It may be the case that students whose majors are not too exacting are precisely the ones who can afford to make the time to be in a fra-ternity and sorority. Nevertheless, this section about Greek life is included so that Latino parents are at least apprised of the realities of college social life.

As Guadalupe Anaya wrote in *The Latino Student's Guide to College Success* (2002),

> "The time you spend in college is a very important part of your life. Some cam-puses have very strong educational or academic reputations, yet others have rep-utations that are non-academic. It is true that some of what you learn in your col-lege years will come from your experiences outside of the classroom. For this reason, college and universities spend a lot to time and money on extracurricu-lar activities and on recreational and cultural programming. Student clubs that are typically found in many high schools are also found on college campuses. Additionally, the town or city may offer many diversions: local festivals, muse-ums, and entertainment. Although this atmosphere is stimulating, students must remember that it is possible to spend too much time on diversions and lose sight of academic and educational goals." (p. 32–33)

Nevertheless, it will be the *socializing* that takes place during the college years that offer some of the most significant glimpses into the world that a college education can give. At a cultural level, this is significant for Latinos. Many Hispanics are guilty of ethnocentrism. They know only their own Latino culture and little else. The privilege of meeting people from cultures that are different from one's own, is what makes college a memorable experience. For Latinos, the added attraction is that college will give them an opportunity to learn about points of view about the world, and all its cultures, that they may not have ever encountered in the *barrio*. Even if Latinos interact with other Latinos on campus, they will get to know other viewpoints from Hispanics who have very different lifestyles and hold diverse opinions about the world. This can be seen as a "loosening up" of the rigid mental *schemata* that Hispanics are raised with. *Schemas* are the lenses through which we see the world and make sense out of everything. They are the set of values, presuppositions, assumptions, and implicit understanding of the world. S*chemas* guide our thinking regarding the causes of events and their sequelae. All of us, no matter what our ethnicity grow up with these *schemas*. Furthermore, our schemas can be very powerful in the way in which they guide our thinking. Many of us will twist facts as to fit them into our schemas so that we can make sense out of our confusing world. For Latinos, these schemas can be very rigid. A very useful and valuable benefit of going to college and being exposed to such different set of ideas and backgrounds is that it allows for a reevaluation of the preconceived notions that one grows up with and allows one to unshackle oneself from certain culturally-bound assumptions which may be self-limiting. In other cases, the reverse may be true. It may cause one to reaffirm certain aspects of one's cultural heritage that not only make sense, but are important to one's self.

As mentioned previously throughout the book, there are certain cultural traits that Latinos must question if they are to succeed in college. By their very nature, Latinos love to socialize, dance, sing, go to parties, drink, and have a good time. This is true of most cultural groups, including Caucasians. However, the extent to which Latinos want to party may be slightly more elevated than the other groups. As Carlota Cardenas De Dwyer wrote in *The Latino Student's Guide to College Success* (2002),

> "One of the most dramatic changes occurring in Latinos' transition to college is that fact that they are leaving the traditional grip of both parents and teachers, as well as other authority figures. For most students, this release triggers an explosion of excessive behavior, particularly on some college campuses where temptations exist in many forms. However, for Latinos, there may be a greater release since most traditional Latino families have strong disciplinarian fathers and mothers with strong religious faith. All these students share one general error in their thinking: that liberty from the restrictions of others implies freedom from the necessity of self-control. " (p. 8)

This makes the situation complex. Latinos do hail from authoritarian and rather conservative households. However, these are also households in which there will be frequent *fiestas* and family gatherings with much beer, food, and music being enjoyed. In a sense, there is a somewhat schizoid combination of patriarchal and Catholic religious conservatism mixed with a tendency to want to have a good time. Nevertheless, De Dwyer (2002) is correct in stating that once Latino students arrive on campus, perhaps that inner tendency to desire getting together and socialize may become even stronger due to the fact that their authoritarian parents are nowhere to be seen. The transition to college will be easier for Latino students who were very studious in high school, and never gave in to excessive amounts of partying or drinking. The self-discipline that Latinos often lack will be more necessary than ever as classes are taken which are intellectually rigorous, demanding much of their time. As De Dwyer (2002) states,

> ". . . a positive attitude and deep determination are required to form a firm conviction that even though not all tasks will be equal, all will be achieved. It could be that a deceptively minor obstruction will require the greatest dedication. Getting up early, staying up late, enduring a forced companionship with an unlikable roommate or instructor, even a visceral dislike of a required subject? all these should be expected at some point and overcome. Each encounter needs to be met with the all-important question to self: Am I going to allow this to stand in my way? Such barriers will halt your progress only if you give up and allow them to do so." (p. 6)

She furthermore adds:

> "Difficult choices will have to be made; old habits and customs may have to changed or put on hold. For example, being prepared to accept the temporary loss of Friday night, Saturday or Sunday afternoon family get-togethers in place of staying in with books or working on a project is a requirement. Over time, recognition that long-term rewards and goals will outweigh short-term losses will provide reassurance to all involved. In college, *academic priorities* must come before recreational or social ones. Only beginning college students themselves can make these difficult choices that demand more than just a willing spirit. Yet the choices are not easy ? you should not begin college with the simple notion that a successful student studies all the time. Indeed, a wise decision reflects more than just the final goal. "Know thyself" expresses the entire collection of vital ingredients that turn the dream of success into reality. " (p. 7)

The other cultural trait that Latinos must keep in check if they are to raise children capable of college material, is the resistance to learning the English language. Only by mastering the English language will Latino students be able to thrive, not just in high school, but to be later able to excel on the entrance exams that will have an influence on whether or not a college or university accepts the applicant. As many parents know, the Scholastic Aptitude Test, or SAT, and the American College Test, or ACT, are both very important in the college application process. The SAT will test a student's reasoning in two main areas: verbal knowledge and mathematics. A corporation known as the College Board writes the policy for the nature and administration of the test. The Educational Testing Service Company, or ETS, prints the test. The ACT is likewise a corporation that writes and prints different types of academic tests. The purpose of the ACT is to indicate a student's ability in verbal skills, mathematical skills, reading comprehension and scientific ability. Both tests will measure a student's ability to reason with, and express himself in, the English language. As De Dwyer (2002) wrote:

> "In English or a verbal section, for example, it would be a major mistake to assume that you would simply recognize the correct answer because it will sound right. In fact, the SAT frequently requires the mental manipulation of many "big ideas," involving distinctions of comparison versus contrast, main idea versus supporting detail, and so on. Similarly, the ACT English test requires students to distinguish between words that serve as a transition and those that serve as supporting details. Both tests demand fine and specific judgments regarding the interpretation of words and ideas, as well as a sound knowledge of English grammar." (p. 16)

Thus, Latino students must have a thorough grounding in the English language if they are to succeed on either the SAT or the ACT. Latino parents must do their part in raising children who will come to know the English language backwards and forward, so that when the time comes for the student to go to college, he or she will have at least one set of skills intact and honed, ready for the necessary demands of college work.

De Dwyer (2002) recommends that students take either the SAT or the ACT in the spring term of the junior year of high school. Seniors in high school can also take the SAT in the fall of their senior year. A good way for students to practice is for them to take the PSAT, or the Preliminary Scholastic Aptitude Test, which can be taken by sophomores and juniors in October.

Yet another way that Latino parents can help their youngsters is to visit a college campus together with them. A campus tour is a wonderful opportunity for an entire family to see the inner workings of a college community. Most college and universities are happy to arrange such tours. Increasingly, high schools, middle schools, and even elementary schools are sending their students onto college campuses on tours so that the students can become familiar with the atmosphere of a college or university. If the school that a Latino student attends does not arrange such tours, the parents can then take the initiative and telephone the colleges and universities they are curious about, and find out when they are giving tours. They are usually coordinated in groups, so the best thing to do to find such a tour is to call the university and to ask for the date and time of the next tour. If they are given on the weekends, which they may be, then the entire family can go. The parents can find such a tour a good way to dispel some of the uncertainties and mysteries of college life. Notable stops and sights on these tours will be the main administration building, the student union, residence dorms, the bookstore, and even some of the classrooms. This will be a wonderful investment of time, and it will certainly begin paving the way for a Latino youngster to make college a reality.

Chapter Nine

Culture & Finances

Culture impacts nearly all areas of life, not the least of which is finances. One might be tempted to dismiss such a notion based on the fact that culture and finances appear, on the surface at least, to be two very different spheres. However, upon closer examination, one finds that finances are inextricably linked to culture. Culture will impact the way that a particular group, or nation, will handle money, business transactions, enterprises, and trade. Certain industries become popularized as part and parcel of a national culture. For instance, eco-tourism in Costa Rica, or the cigar manufacturing businesses in Cuba, to name only two. There are times when a country's entire image is put behind a product in order to be able to sustain its economy. This is especially true if the product is a major export.

For Latinos in the United States, however, the situation is a bit gloomier. It has been said that we are now living in a new "hourglass" economy. Simply put, the hourglass economy implies that there are two big "bubbles" in the American economy. This means that there are those at the "bottom" and those at the "top." Those in the bottom bubble are the low-wage manual laborers, blue-collar workers, and industrial employees who work for a bare subsistence. As has been mentioned amply throughout this book, Latinos currently face one of the highest poverty rates of any ethnic group in the United States. Hispanics occupy the bottom bubble of the hourglass economy in America. On a basic level, the economy of California as well as much of the entire U.S. Southwest is built around the importation of cheap labor from Latin America. Many agricultural businesses benefit from having inexpensive labor that it can then exploit. Anyone who does not believe that this exploitation occurs in the United States is being unrealistic. There are huge tracts of land in the Southwest, and especially in California, which rely upon migrant labor. Not only does agriculture benefit from cheap labor, but so do many other sectors of the American economy. Most restaurants, hotels, and many other entertainment establishments benefit from having this large influx of cheap, replaceable labor from Latin America. It is no surprise to anyone that many of these laborers are undocumented. Employers benefit because they do not have to pay for medical insurance benefits, or 401k retirement plans. Nor do they have to obey minimum wage laws. From the businesses' point of view, the less they have to pay for wages, the better. From the point of view of the employee, it is a ready source of available tax-free income. Additionally, another benefit to the employee is that the jobs are simple, demand little education, and little flexibility of talents. California's produce industry relies on illegal labor from Mexico and Latin America. In order for an employee to move up into the upper bubble of the hourglass economy in the United States, he or she would have to attain a high level of education, fluency in English, and have both mental acuity and intellectual flexibility. The hourglass economy is unlikely to change in the immediate future. It benefits both employees and employers.

A downside to this arrangement, one of many, is that it keeps Latinos locked into the laboring classes in America. As long as Latinos are uneducated and fail to earn a college degree, or even graduate from high school, they will continue to occupy the bottom level of the economy. Another unfortunate consequence of this situation is that employers and business owners reduce the amount money going to the IRS in the form of as undeclared personal income taxes from the undocumented workers, much of which could be rerouted back to these employers and business owners in the form of federal grants or subsidies.

Another reason why this hourglass metaphor is effective is that it shows how the narrow "neck" of the hourglass represents middle management, or middle-level employees. This narrow corridor leads upward to the top bubble that is populated by the corporate executives. It also leads downward to the laboring class in the bottom bubble. Thus, the elites occupy a large bubble, as do the low-wage laborer. Only a selected few will be able to rise from the bottom bubble up into the narrow neck and become middle managers. Fewer still will rise from the middle region and ascend to the top bubble. With Latinos continuing to drop out of high school, and not completing their education, the situation is unlikely to improve for them. They will continue to occupy the bottom bubble of the hourglass economy.

Another way in which Latinos adversely impact their personal finances with regard to the educational future of their children is the large financial contributions, in the form of remittances, that are sent yearly by families living in the United States down to their relatives in Mexico. *What Latinos do not realize is that if they were to only use their limited financial means to send their children to college in the United States, these future college-educated professionals could use their higher wage-earning capabilities to help their families here and in Mexico. Proportionally, this financial assistance would represent less of a sacrifice by those providing it, by virtue of their higher salaries.*

According to a recent article, $16.6 billion dollars flowed from the United States down to Mexico in 2004. These billions were mostly from remittances sent by immigrant families down to their compatriots in Mexico. This is a huge sum that could be used for other purposes, not the least of which could be to finance a college education. This article then went to state that, on average, $1,600 is sent in remittances by the average Mexican immigrant to family members in Mexico. That same $1,600 could be used, the author stated, to cover the tuition at one of the California State Universities. The author also stated that, in California, only 10 percent of Hispanic children will obtain a college degree. Additionally, only 25 percent of all ethnic groups will obtain a college degree. Furthermore, this writer stated that although over 40 percent of migrants do not have health insurance, many insurance companies have plans that can cover a family for less than $200 a month.

What is occurring is a cultural dynamic in which Latinos are supposed to be communal and family-centered. Yet, this family-centeredness is costing Latinos money, the opportunity to have adequate health insurance coverage, and the opportunity to send their children to college. This is another example of the cultural incompatibility between classical Latino culture and the rugged individualism of Anglo-Protestant American culture. The Anglo-Protestant culture bases its success, in part, in the attainment of a higher education. If Hispanics were to begin thinking about their own families in the United States and less about those in Mexico or any other home country of origin, they would realize that this money could be used for their betterment. More students in the family could be sent to college or university and go on to have good careers and more family members could be covered by health insurance if less money were to be sent back to their home country. This goes to show the blind adherence to cultural traditions in Hispanic families that have kept Latinos at a perpetual disadvantage for some many generations in the United States. The rugged individualism that has been one of the corner-stones of American culture must be embraced in order for Hispanics to be able to reap some of the gains that Anglo Americans have realized over time. What this also points to in the Latino community is a cultural persistence on living only for the present moment. Thus, if a family member in Mexico, or any other Latin American nation, calls on a family member living in the United States and asks for money, because he or she needs it, the family member in the United States will think only of that moment and send as much money as he or she can afford to send to Mexico. Unfortunately, this represents a misconception that relatives living in Latin America have of the financial status of their compatriots living in the United States; they think that the relatives in America have all the money in the world to send in remittances. They believe that relatives in the United States have few expenses and large salaries. Sadly, the opposite is usually true.

What if a Mexican American child living in Los Angeles without health insurance were to come down with appendicitis? If his parents have been sending hundreds of dollars home, over time, to Mexico, then that child's life will literally be at risk. All of this could happen as a result of sending remittances to Mexico instead of using that money to obtain adequate health insurance for a child in the United States. Instead, many uninsured and undocumented individuals take advantage of the emergency room. This rightly angers many health care workers who feel that many immigrants come here only for free emergency health care, such as baby deliveries, without paying into the system themselves. Latinos continue to believe that sending remittances to their countries of origin is their duty and that asking the American government for assistance makes good sense. As Hanson (2003) points out, "Welfare, disability, workman's compensation, Head Start, Social Security, Medicare, Medicaid, supplemental assistance—all that largess (and the availability of cheap Chinese-produced goods) has a created a real consumer class from the immigrant community, the unemployed and the half-employed—while this newfound affluence has made them, in a way, angrier that they are not as wealthy as others." (p. 131–132)

Latinos must change the way they view money. It must be viewed as a more precious commodity, and not sent so freely home to their native countries, in the form of remittances, or spent on useless consumer products. Latinos can use a variety of ways to save money. One way is for Latinos to abandon some of their rather materialistic tastes. As mentioned previously in an earlier chapter, there exists in the Hispanic community an expensive love of throwing fiestas, as well as elaborate *quinceneras*. For Hispanic males, there is also a love of modified vintage muscle cars, which are also quite expensive. Although exact figures are difficult to compute, the average cost of an elaborate party with prodigious quantities of food and alcohol, and perhaps even a disc jockey, can be quite expensive for a poor Latino family living in a ghetto or *barrio*. One wanders if, on a psychological level, they throw parties so as to forget their poverty. However, they end up shooting themselves in the foot; these costly fiestas, quinceaneras, and muscle cars drive them deeper into the money pit. The quincenera dress, for example, is expensive, worn only once, and thrown into the back of the closet. For Hispanic males, especially those domiciled in poor neighborhoods, the purchase of an elaborate vintage sedan, which is modified with a stronger engine, very expensive chrome wheels, and an elaborate set of speakers, represents what must be a very large financial investment. These are the same individuals who are preparing fast food at mini-malls for a living. Of course, they are working at these fast-food franchises because they do not possess the education to find more meaningful employment. The reason for their low-wage employment can be traced directly to their lack of a degree as well as the critical thinking skills necessary for the attainment of a better job. Most of their wages go towards the upkeep of their cars. They lock themselves in to a low-level job, which pays minimum wage, and they cannot rise any higher. It is almost as if the message is: "I don't care if I'm poor and uneducated, as long as I have this set of wheels, I'm a real *hombre*."

Related to this phenomenon, is the Hispanic cultural tendency to live only for the moment. This was also mentioned in an earlier chapter. The very same families who throw these elaborate quinceaneras or these individuals who buy their muscles are living only for the momentary gratification that having those things will bring. They are not investing their money in an education for the future. In Mexico, there is a widespread cultural perception, especially among the poorer classes, that if one is quick enough, and clever enough, one can peddle a product or service and strike it rich. Why should one invest in the future if one can get lucky? There are those who have been fortunate enough to develop a product or service, or even a recipe, which allows them to strike it rich. In the United States, there are some stories that celebrate similar successes, such as Bill Gates, who dropped out of Harvard and later founded his Microsoft empire. However, in Mexico, the perception is widespread that if you can get into business with the right individuals, or peddle the right product at just the right time, you can make it, or at least get by and avoid going to college. Mexican families migrating into the United States transplant that belief. Thus, their offspring, although born in America, are still under the Mexican cultural impression that if they just work hard enough, and fast enough, they can rise up without having to go to college. Of course, the personal growth enhancing benefits of going to college are also ignored. That is a notion that is too abstract for the Latino mind to grasp. Rather, the emphasis is on making a "quick buck." No one enjoys poverty, and it is only natural and even commendable, that if a person is facing a financially difficult situation, that he or she will do everything that is possible to improve that situation. But for Latinos, the attempts at making money quickly, and trying to be smart enough and entrepreneurial enough, to become successful without having to go to college, is hurting them more than helping them.

For many young Latinos, this begins at the age of eighteen. Reaching eighteen years of age is an important stage for all adolescents in the United

States, regardless of their ethnic group. However, Latino adolescents are particularly prone to feel that they have come of age and are now free to do anything, which is, in a sense, correct. Latino eighteen-year olds will tend to feel more independent and will want to do more things on their own than they could have before. At eighteen, one becomes a *young man*, or a *young woman*, and as such, the world is supposed to open up to them. Many Hispanic adolescents have already been working by the time they reach eighteen. The satisfying feeling, which is very basic and intrinsic, of earning a paycheck through one's own efforts, and having money to spend, becomes addictive and intoxicating to them. For many Hispanic youngsters, finishing high school and being able to go to a job, and maintaining steady employment, has an appeal that is inescapable. Personal growth, the reading of books, and the development of an understanding of the world, is no longer important to Latino adolescents at that point. The sad thing is that Hispanic adolescents might profess how important it is to go to college, and perhaps some of them may carry a class or two at the local community college, but in reality, their hearts are not invested in the total experience of college.

Independence becomes a paradox for these Hispanic adolescents. For many of these young adults, independence implies merely financial emancipation from their parents through working and earning a living. True independence of thought is an entirely different phenomenon unknown to them. Being able to earn a living means more to them than anything else. They are eighteen, legal, can marry, or become parents. They feel they can do whatever they want. Yet their minds are just as closed and narrow as ever before. For many of these young Latinos, there is no shame in low-skill or menial work. Nor should there be. Yet, there is little effort made to become exceptional or high-achieving individuals.

What pervades this entire culture of turning eighteen and doing whatever one wants, is that there seems to be little focus on personally meaningful experiences, which could be termed as inner-focused, personally profound, enriching, or even spiritual. For Latinos, maintaining their so-called personal independence and settling for minimum-wage earnings, is more important to them than growth-enhancing experiences, many of which cost little, or may even be free. These are the same Latino youngsters, who along with their parents, during a Catholic Mass, are looking around, talking, giggling, fumbling through their purses, or checking their cell phones, and doing everything except praying. The minds of these Latinos are so focused on the outer, the car, the boom box, the camera cell phone, and the almighty dollar, that there is little energy left to focus on self-improvement. This discussion should not divert attention from the fact that at times it becomes necessary to focus on outer realities, such as one's career. Being able to hold steady employment is very important, especially when one is responsible for others, such as young children. It is through meaningful work that one can find some of life's greatest pleasure and gratification. However, finding one's most effective niche in the career market takes time, effort, diligence, and a focus inward. This inner-focus is where Latino culture has failed. Latino culture focuses only on the immediate, physical, tangible, and the *outer layer*. Hispanic culture leaves Hispanics with little capacity for self-evaluation, inner growth, self-directed activities, and personally meaningful quests.

Another prime example of how living only for the moment is ultimately harmful to Latinos is the fact that many older, or elderly, Latino couples living in the United States, speaking little English, are living in poverty after many years of earning only a subsistence standard of life. They end up poor in their old age and perhaps in poor health as well. That is perhaps one of the most tragic consequences of a life spent living only for the moment. For many Hispanics in the United States, time catches up, and they find themselves older, less able, and depending on perhaps both the American government and their grown children for financial and Spanish-English translation. This is why Latinos should begin to understand the consequences of their life choices as well as the consequences of not going to college. That is not to say that going to college is a panacea that will magically arrange all of one's life conditions forever and anon. Rather, college gives one the tools with which to begin living a life that has purpose, goals, and a set of values that are ultimately more in line with what works in the United States. Thus, the need to focus on planning for the future needs to begin much earlier, preferably when Latinos are in their early teen years.

Yet another factor that is affecting Latinos' ability to go to college and make a brighter future for themselves is the fact that many of them, especially their immigrant parents, mistakenly believe that college is too expensive. They believe that the tuition is out of their reach. What many Hispanic parents must realize is that there is a great deal of financial aid available for aspiring college students. Scholarships and grants are monies available to students and do not have to be repaid. Loans do have to be repaid; however, what Latinos must understand is that the long-term return on their college investment is more than worth the amount borrowed and the interest paid on a government loan. This once again points to the Latino tendency to focus only on the present. They see the loan for college not as an investment in the future, but as a financial setback. There is almost a distrust of the process of obtaining a Stafford loan to pay for college. This is a certain irony in this, since Latinos think nothing of appealing to the federal government for other forms of financial assistance. Why they don't feel comfortable in obtaining a loan to help pay for college is somewhat of a paradox.

There are other things Hispanics can begin doing for themselves in this realm, such as reading more literature on scholarships, grants, and loans. This will familiarize them to the process and benefits of applying, thereby eliminating some of the mystery surrounding financial aid.

Unfortunately, one of the most insidious ways in which Latinos become victims of their own ignorance and poverty is through the act of giving money to scam artists, charlatans, and other unscrupulous individuals who take advantage of poor, uneducated and excessively trusting people. This is a classic example where culture, lack of education, ignorance and money all combine to make a huge market of health-related products, mostly herbal remedies or relics, geared for Hispanics which are supposed to carry magical cures, or magical properties, special powers, or endow the possessor with telepathic or telekinetic capabilities. If Latinos do not become more educated, they will continue to fall prey to these same scam artists. I once watched a television commercial for a medallion, which, if the good-natured Latino purchaser of it were to place the medallion under the bed, all sorts of good fortune would befall him or her. The benefits were to include finding love, marriage, financial freedom, and occupational success. Not only have Latinos made themselves victims of exploitation with all sorts of harsh working conditions, they have also made themselves ripe for exploitation for the modern snake oil vendor, due to their ignorance. Other products that I have seen advertised on the Hispanic, as well as American, channels, include magical creams that are supposed to help women shed away pounds by the mere act of lathering their legs and thighs with this product. Heaven knows what other products are sold to unsuspecting Latino television watchers.

It is time for Hispanics to awaken to the fact that there are scam artists and charlatans ready, willing, and able to make money off their ignorance by selling them products of pure fakery. Latinos must realize that their lifestyle focuses only on the present moment and how much their lives will begin to improve by planning more for the future. They must plan for a college education for themselves, and for their children.

Chapter Ten

Practical Advice for Parents

One of the most important things parents can do is to instill in their children the optimal emotional, intellectual, and cultural assets that will enable their children to succeed in school and eventually succeed in college. The idea behind this *academic resilience* is that, although all students eventually face setbacks in school, they will nevertheless possess a sturdiness of character that will allow them not only to withstand the setbacks, but also to persevere and excel in their studies. The question becomes: How does one inculcate this quality in a child? A very basic way in which a child can be made to feel motivated to succeed in school is if the child feels that he or she has a unique talent that can be channeled into an academic pursuit. Some children have an artistic streak, and may be best suited for studying creative writing, the Arts, or even a field such as graphic design, which is computerized yet incorporates a person's creative vision. Other children have a propensity for analytical thinking. For these children, a pursuit of the Sciences may be their best avenue of future career exploration.

It is important that parents collaborate with teachers in spotting the special strengths, aptitudes, and abilities inherent in each child. Motivation is not created in a vacuum. Rather, it is the natural byproduct of when a person knows for certain that he or she has something special to contribute to the world. In my own journey of writing the book, I felt motivated by my keen and sincere wish to help Latinos with their education. It has become my life's work. It is my calling. Parents need to develop in their child the feeling that he or she has a unique calling or special mission.

Following is a list of practical tips that readers can use to inspire either their own children, or an at-risk student that a reader may know, to succeed in school:

1. Parents should sit down with their child every day after school to find out how his or her day has unfolded. This will allow parents to spot that which engages their child's attention the most in school. Only in talking to their child will parents be able to understand what their child finds most interesting, and what is, of course, least interesting.

2. Notice the actual grades on the report cards that are brought home from school. By spotting a pattern, if any, parents will be able to spot strengths and aptitudes. The key is to build on the strengths.

3. Low grades occur when they are allowed to occur. Set the highest standards possible. Do not allow low grades to be even an option. I can almost guarantee that if a child is raised in a home where low grades are not even a consideration, then low grades will not manifest themselves.

4. Encourage good grades by rewarding exemplary schoolwork. The best rewards are words of praise, enthusiasm and physical affection from the parents. The words of encouragement that a child hears will have a strong influence. Simple phrases such as "Great job!" or "I'm so proud of you" followed by a hug can work wonders in building a child's sense of self-worth and motivation.

5. Simply put, privileges such as web surfing or downloading music from the Internet should be the reward that a child gets to enjoy after having studied and completed his or her homework.

6. Make sure the homework is not only completed, but that it is of the highest quality.

7. Homework time should be fixed and unwavering. Children can collaborate with their parents in agreeing to which time slot they will devote to homework. Some children need to unwind with physical activity after a full day of being in school; others can buckle down right away and take advantage of the momentum of the previous six or seven hours of sitting in a classroom. Parents need to be aware of their child's "peak time" to study.

8. It is crucial that parents create the right atmosphere for study. No child will be able to concentrate with blaring music or the rapid-fire images of television illuminating the living room, or even with the back-and-forth yelling from room to room that is common in so many homes. During the agreed-upon study time, parents need to enforce the rule that all distracting stimuli be eliminated. In practical terms, shut off the television, loud music, and even appliances. However, some students are able to focus better if they have particular types of music playing softly in the background. Soft instrumental and classical music may enhance a student's focus.

9. Make certain that there is a healthy supply of the materials that may be needed for all types of school assignments. Lined and unlined school

paper, rulers, compasses, pens, pencils, erasers, highlighters, colored markers, crayons, and white-out are all necessary supplies. As mentioned in the instructional tapes "Where There's a Will, There's an A," a sturdy basket or plastic crate, available for a low price from any Wal-Mart or K-Mart, can make the study area and time more efficient. These are compact and portable and are a boon to students who are at a babysitter's house before their parents pick them up. If a child does his or her homework at the babysitter's, then the basket or crate can travel with them. This will curtail the excuses students typically use to justify incomplete or untouched homework. The usage of a portable supply container encourages responsibility.

10. Parents need to differentiate between involvement and assuming responsibility that belongs to the child. Being highly involved in a child's education does not translate into doing their homework for them. With regard to homework, there is a difference between supervising and doing. This boils down to the division of roles and the responsibilities that stem from those roles. It is a student's responsibility to complete all schoolwork. But it is also a parent's responsibility to make sure that it is done well. In addition, it is the parent's duty to monitor and enforce the rules regarding study time and expectations. Parents are also responsible for the allocation or withholding of privileges based upon the performance of a child.

11. Close ties must be maintained with a child's teachers, thus allowing parents to know how, and when, school assignments are supposed to be completed. Supervision of homework is thus more thorough. If a parent understands that a child has to do the *odd-numbered math problems* and show his or her work, then they can hold the child to that standard. The parents themselves need to understand the standard that they are enforcing. This can only be accomplished by having the parents maintaining a close collaboration with the child's teachers.

12. Even when there is no homework assigned, a child should still review his or her notes from that day's classes. The student can then use his or her regular study time to plan and organize future assignments. This will allow the student to develop the lifelong skill of *managing assignments*, which can be utilized not only during the college years, but also in the workplace. Students need to know in advance how to prepare for an upcoming assignment and be able to divide it into manageable segments that they can work on in advance. This allows students and their parents to avoid the nightmare of a hastily arranged, last-minute scramble the night before an assignment is due.

13. Make *reading* a true family value. Parents should require their children

to read every day. When they are very small, children will incorporate the habit of reading by watching their parents read books. As they get older, this should be encouraged further. Reading daily will help a student to become more proficient at math word problems. The practice of reading helps develop the capacity in the young child's mind to process information. In addition, reading is the means through which the child understands how the world works. From history to politics to economics, only through reading will all of these areas of the world make sense to a child. Only a student who reads books as a matter of course will be able to navigate successfully through his school and college years. Reading promotes a strong vocabulary and proper grammar usage. In the business world, employees are penalized if they cannot write a formal business letter. One cannot even be considered for a job interview if one's resume is poorly written. Thus, strong English skills are valued highly in the "real world." Reading thus becomes a form of empowerment through the information that is gained.

14. Every grade and every mark that a child receives should be linked in his or her mind with a goal. That is to say, the child should not view an "A" in a vacuum. Rather, it should been seen as something necessary to progress to the next grade or into the next school. In a very real sense, high marks are the mortar between the bricks being laid in an upward progression as a child advances through grade school, high school, and then college. Parents need to show not only positive encouragement but to continuously remind a child that whatever high grade he or she receives sets the stage for progression. The drive to earn high marks in grade school will sow the seed for ambition in later life. Ambition and drive have to be fostered when a child is young. In the end, it is ambition that allows educated persons to become successful in life. This is a quality conspicuously absent in certain segments of the Latino community.

15. Set a time limit on the amount of television, video gaming, and Internet usage that a child gets to engage in each day. However, do not enforce this time limit in a vacuum. Rather, the child should view these finite leisure activities as the privilege and reward for a job well done in school that day up to and including homework. The link has to be made in the child's mind between the work they do and the privileges they get to enjoy. This becomes the model for how society functions. Society, as a rule, rewards not only hard work, but also high quality work. No employee will receive a promotion in the business world for mediocre work. What parents do by allowing, for example, one hour of web surfing for a job well done in school, homework, or a test, will prime a child to link effort to reward.

16. Parents must enforce the rules together. Nothing can undermine parental authority more quickly than having one parent be the "heavy," which will cause the children to win over the other "softy" and use every manipulation necessary to get the "softy" to agree to suspend the rules "just this once" and essentially subvert the harmony that should exist between a mother and father. Additionally, cooperation and mutual enforcement between Mommy and Daddy create a psychological firewall in the child's mind. It leaves a vivid impression in the child that he or she cannot, and should not, attempt to "beat the system." Before infants even enroll in a school, the parents need to agree together beforehand what rules will be laid down and how. Even when the child is in the middle of adolescence, the parents should talk to each other at night, away from the children, and come to an agreement on how they will enforce the rules mutually and cooperatively. They have to agree together on both the rewards as well as the punishments. This underscores the need for clear and mutually respectful communication between the parents. It is crucial that these sessions, when parents strategize, be private. Otherwise the children will catch on to the disharmony and exploit it. Latino husbands need to take great care not to undermine their wives authority over the children by acquiescing to the children's demands. This makes the mother the "heavy," and that is one of the biggest grievances that mothers have against their husbands. Hispanics wives also need to communicate clearly to their husbands the cooperation that they will need from them.

17. Although it may seem obvious and like common sense, a child needs to attend classes regularly in order to absorb the material that is presented during class lectures. There are many Latino parents, especially Mexican parents, who feel that it is more important that the child attend to a family farm in Mexico rather than attend class in a school in the United States. This is more prevalent in the Border States. The damaging aspect of this cultural practice is the fact that it sends the message that parents are not partners in the educational process of their child. Furthermore, it sends the message that education is not that important. A friend of mine has a son who became very ill and missed two weeks of school. His teacher informed her that even missing two weeks due to illness can cause a serious setback and conveyed to her, in effect, that good grades are contingent upon attendance. It becomes very difficult for a student to catch up with the rest of the class if he or she has missed many days of school. Much energy is expended in merely catching up rather than being at the forefront of the class.

18. High expectations eventually equate to high achievement. I once had a friend in college who was Korean American. One day, while sitting on a

bench on the campus of Long Beach City College, I asked him how he managed to always get good grades in college. He told me very simply, "I never settled for less than the best." Parental expectations should be no different than what my friend conveyed to me. Latino parents should expect nothing less than the very best that their children have to offer. Simply put, average performance is the result of average expectations.

19. Parents and students should collaborate in the effort to keep all school assignments and meetings organized. One way is by keeping a large calendar with all of the important dates posted in an area that is highly visible, such as a refrigerator door. School assignments, term papers, science fair projects, PTA meetings, and progress reports should all be listed well in advance of their due dates, so that nothing is completed at the last minute, or neglected entirely.

20. A direct line of communication needs to be kept open between parents and the school. Parents need to ask every day whether there is anything for them from the school in their child's backpack. All too often, the school will send home mailers, letters, announcements, or worse, notices regarding academic problems, and these are left "mysteriously" undelivered.

21. Some schools maintain a system of communication with the parents through written notes. Latino parents may want to take advantage of this form of communication. It is not dependent on technology. It is free, and efficient. Even if such a system is not in place at the school, parents should request progress notes from their child's teacher, and they should not hesitate to ask for them even on a daily basis during critical times.

22. Students should prepare themselves for school every night by organizing all of their materials, assignments, folders, and school supplies. This will allow the student to become efficient in the way he or she approaches his or her school day.

23. When a student is given a list of assignments for homework, he or she should tackle them by prioritizing the work, starting with the most difficult. It is only natural that some assignments will be more difficult than others. What students should do when they come home each day is to evaluate the assignments and do the hardest assignment first.

24. Parents may want to keep the energy flowing in the study time of their child or children by keeping a ready supply of natural food snacks. A bowl of fruit or granola bars would be good sources of energy for the child's brain, providing fuel for the task of doing several hours worth of work.

25. Some children might benefit from either physical exercise or a power nap after school. This would allow their minds and bodies to recover from a

full day at school. If they were to begin doing their homework right after school, they may not be giving themselves time to recuperate from sitting in class lectures all day. The mind needs breaks. So does the body. The form that this break takes varies from day to day. So on some days an hour's swim at the municipal swimming pool may provide the release that they crave after sitting still for many hours, whereas on other days sleeping for an hour may be what they require. Parents should encourage their children to let them know what they need by way of sleep or exercise.

26. From a very young age, the expectation on the part of the parents to have their son or daughter go to college should already be in place. It should not even be a source of wonderment or debate. The question becomes: *which* college will my son or daughter attend? This will have to be worked out amongst the family members. Cost, location, religious preferences, and even the campus culture will all factor into the decision as to which college a student should attend. Nevertheless, the expectations should be firmly in place that college will be part of that young person's future regardless of which college is chosen.

27. Another way in which standards can become manifest is through personal appearance. Many public school districts have already implemented standards of academic dress through uniforms. Implementing uniforms eliminates competition and holds everyone to the same conservative standard of dress. In schools where there is no such uniform, parents must exercise a high level of caution by setting their own standards for the way their child may or may not dress for school. The way in which a child dresses will reflect, to a certain extent, the values of the home. Spiked hair, spiked gloves, and choke collars all say something of the home from which that child hails. Parents should feel comfortable "laying down the law" as to what a child may or may not wear at home and in school. The values of the home will eventually become manifest at school, and from the school these values will be reflected in the community. The values of the community in turn will impact on households. It becomes a closed circle of values.

28. Parents can greatly enhance the study period for their child by opening their home, selectively, to allow the more motivated students to study together with their child. The students will benefit from a sense of belonging to a motivated circle of friends. It can ease the feeling of isolation while studying and allow them to feel valued by other members of their peer group. By doing this, parents can keep a check on the values which influence the peer group interactions of their child. Thus, instead of gathering in the middle of the street to talk about hot rods and smoking cigarettes, youngsters can enjoy interacting with their peers and yet those interactions remain under the healthy influence of their parents' emphasis

on academic ambition.

29. Children need sleep, plain and simple. Young bodies need to recover from all the energy they have expended. Thus, bedtime needs to be fixed and unwavering. Parents can win the bedtime battles by not allowing themselves to be "taken in" by the entreaties of their child who begs and begs and pleads and whines to get Mommy to let him or her stay up "just this once." If it's a television show that they want to watch, it can be videotaped. If it's the academy awards or the Super Bowl, they can read about it the next day in the newspaper. This will encourage students to read rather than view a newsworthy item on television. Furthermore, anything that is very newsworthy, such as a war or late-breaking news, can be turned into an academic discussion through printed media such as books and newspaper articles. Instead of having a child watch the news until 11 p.m., parents can find newspaper clippings and magazine articles and these can be given as supplemental academic material to be discussed at the dinner table. However, given the brutal nature of some of the stories making headlines while this is in print, it is advisable that parents take precautionary measures to screen the stories that they allow children to read or discuss at the dinner table.

30. Parents can make the weekends an extension of their child's weekday education by taking children to museums, concerts, symphonies, and art exhibits to supplement what they are learning during the week. Ideally, these activities will be age-appropriate and interactive. A trip to a museum can work wonders in allowing a child to learn, for instance, how lightning is created, or to touch a meteorite that has traveled through outer space for millions of years, or to look through an observatory telescope and see stars that are emitting light from other galaxies. Museums and their exhibits are the links where textbook facts connect to the real world in dynamic and entertaining ways.

31. Parents need to take time to explain the rationale behind each of these ideas that have been mentioned above. Their values cannot and should not exist in a vacuum. An entire family will benefit from open and honest dialogue that reveals the reasoning behind each of these rules, expectations, and proscriptions. The goal is to have the child internalize these values. This may not happen right away, and there will be times when the child will not want to cooperate. A child's values may be, on some level, at odds with those of his parents. Good values need to be enforced consistently and strongly. Ultimately, most parents want the good values of their home to sink into their child's mind. However, this should not be done with "an iron fist." Instead, these good values should be promoted within in an atmosphere of love, warmth, caring, and patience.

32. It may be obvious, but the child's performance will be aided by having the child get to school on time every day. Alarm clocks are very cheap, and they can be one of the most important tools used at home. Parents must see to it that their child or children get to school with adequate time to spare. If a child is to arrive late to school, the teacher or staff should receive notice ahead of time either through a telephone call or a written note from the parents along with a number at which the parents can be reached. This last detail is to prevent children from forging a parental note. Lastly, even before a school year begins, it is the responsibility of the parents to make sure that adequate transportation will be available for the child during the entire school year.

33. At the start of the school year, the parents should make the effort to meet all of the child's teachers. No doubt, these teachers will have different personalities, backgrounds, beliefs, and teaching methods. Parents should be prepared for this plurality of personalities in the school. They must retain an open mind when meeting these teachers. First impressions may prove erroneous with time. One of the most powerful linkages in a child's education will be this close relationship between the parents and the teaching staff at the school. Only through this close contact will parents be alerted to problems, either academic or behavioral in nature. Parents or legal guardians can respond more quickly to exigencies, such as a sudden onset of flu symptoms in the child, if they are in close contact with the school.

34. At the end of the school day, the child should have adequate transportation to either their home or another parent-authorized location. "Latch-key" children with an inordinate amount of unsupervised and unstructured time are the ones most at risk to experiment with drugs or sex. These are also the children whose peer groups can have a disastrous effect.

These are only a handful of suggestions. Parents can, and should, be as creative as possible in finding of maintaining high standards, while at the same time conveying the message to their children that education can be pleasure-filled experience. If the home environment only enforces discipline and rules, then that atmosphere will kill the very spirit and flame that must be kindled if education is to be enjoyed. A child must be given the chance to discover the pleasure of learning, and the wonder of discovery, which, of course, ought to be at the base of every child's educational experience.

Chapter Eleven

Academic Resilience

This chapter will deal with one of the most important factors involved in student success, academic resilience. How do we define academic resilience? First, we must ask: What is resilience? Resilience can be loosely defined as the ability to persist and endure under general conditions of duress or negative life circumstances. It is also an extremely valuable psychological tool. Resilience is what will allow people to withstand the most difficult of life's circumstances. This is what allows people to achieve their goals despite setbacks, or despite some disappointments.

We can further loosely define resilience to say that it is *strength in action*. The person that displays resilience, or resiliency, is displaying the ability to withstand an external negative event, or negative agent, and yet be able to show the ability to make continued efforts at whatever goal or success that has been identified as the desideratum. The reason that this internal, or psychological, factor needs to be studied is the fact that it plays a major role in the ability of the student to graduate successfully despite negative life events. It appears as if certain minority groups, especially Hispanics, have been more prone to succumb to these negative life events more so than others. It also appears that these events will have a major impact upon their educational success. Pidcock, Fischer, and Munsch (2001), citing research by Eagle & Carroll (1988), and Wechsler et al. (1994), found that ". . . 80% of all Hispanic undergraduates leave college without graduating." (p. 803) Furthermore, "Among high school graduates, the percentage of Hispanics who eventually earn a bachelor's degree has been noted to be roughly one-third that of Anglos." (p. 803) Furthermore, it appears that resiliency may be more important during certain stages, or certain periods, of a young person's education. Pidcock, Fischer and Munsch (2001) found that, "For the Hispanic students, the freshman year represented an opportunity for both vulnerability and resiliency to risk factors to be expressed in their level of academic success." (p. 809)

How does one develop academic resilience? The answer to this question is complex and multifaceted. It is also somewhat theory-dependent. In her book, *The Unmotivated Child* (1996), Natalie Rathvon, Ph.D., explains the difficulty that many students have in persisting with their schoolwork from the perspective of Attachment Theory. This theory refers to the way in which children are able to develop either a secure or insecure attachment to an adult authority figure. The child who is raised with loving, supportive parents develops a secure attachment to authority figures and will see them as helpful and responsive to his needs. The child who grows up being mistreated or neglected will come to view authority figures as those who are unresponsive and hurtful to his needs. As Rathvon explains, "For children to develop secure attachments, [the parents] must be able to satisfy two basic needs. First, they must feel safe and cared for, and second, they must feel supported and validated in their efforts to explore their world." (p. 13) However, as she points out, some children grow up with parents who themselves were not given the kind of secure attachments that they needed when they were children. Thus, many children grow up being raised by parents who themselves have an insecure attachment both within themselves and the external world. The most crucial point to emphasize is that as a child grows up, his efforts at independent exploration must be encouraged. As Rathvon explains it,

> "If the child's efforts to achieve security and to explore his world are acknowledged and validated by the parent, he develops a sense of self-efficacy. But if his efforts to find a secure base or to explore beyond it are often ignored, discouraged, or modified to meet the parent's needs rather than his own, the child comes to believe that it does not matter what he does . . . it is logical for him to disavow responsibility for events in the outer world, including his own behavior. Instead, he assigns responsibility to persons or events outside himself." (p. 66–67)

What this means is that as an infant is beginning to crawl on the floor and explore his world, the parents must make every effort to encourage his independent exploration. The baby's ability to explore his or her world will become internalized and a sense of mastery and exploratory control will later be internalized and used in his adult life. In adult terms, this is known as an *internal locus of control*. This means that one has internalized the center of control and responsibility for one's actions within oneself. Someone with an internal locus of control knows that he or she is basically responsible for the events that occur in his or her world, and has had some role to play in both positive and negative events that occur. However, this center of control has its origins in the way that a baby is allowed to explore his world. This allows the mind of the infant to begin to feel a sense of mastery in that exploration. As Rathvon (1996), explains it,

> "When in the course of [the infant's] exploration he encounters something new or difficult, he calmly examines the obstacles that stand in the way of solving the problem, devises strategies for overcoming them, and continues to try, secure in the belief that his persistence will ultimately be rewarded." (p. 70)

This persistence that she refers to is what we have defined as being one of the central ingredients in academic resilience. Is it really that simple? Is it really a matter of raising a child since infancy with an environment that allows safe and calm exploration so that the child grows up confident in his or her ability to develop a sense of exploratory mastery? Perhaps it is *not* that simple. Gutman and Midgley (2000) hypothesized that the interplay between protective factors is the most effective combination likely to ensure resilience in at least some populations of students. These researchers referenced Garmezy (1993) who found three groups of factors that seem to operate protectively for students:

> "... (a) psychological factors, such as perceived academic competence, (b) characteristics of the family context such as involved parenting, and (c) the availability of external support systems, as exemplified by a supportive teacher or an institutional structure such as a caring school environment." (p. 225)

Gutman and Midgley (2000) further broke down the different spheres of psychological factors, family factors, school factors, and the interplay between multiple protective factors. When researching psychological factors, Bandura (1986); Compas, (1987); Garmezy (1983, 1991, 1993); Harter (1990); Lord, Eccles and McCarthy (1994) found that "Problem-solving skills, cognitive skills, confidence in one's competence, and feelings of efficacy are key influences on one's adjustment to stressful situations." (As referenced by Gutman and Midgley, 2000, p.226.) Furthermore, Clark (1983); Tienda and Kao (1994); found that

> "High achieving . . . poor African American adolescents have parents who are more involved in their education both within the home (e.g., conversations with their adolescents about school and consistent monitoring of organized learning activities) and at school (e.g., frequent contact with the school initiated by parents and attendance at PTSA meetings)." (As referenced by Gutman and Midgley, 2000, p.226)

The research of Gutman and Midgley highlighted the importance of school factors in their interplay with the other internal factors mentioned previously.

By school factors, we may refer to such things as having teachers express their concern to at-risk students, spending time with those students after school, meeting with the students' parents often, and having a staff at the school which makes parents feel welcome and encouraged to participate. This last point is particularly crucial for parents whose first language is not English, especially Hispanics. It is important that schools have a fully bilingual staff that can accommodate and encourage Spanish-speaking parents to come to the school and meet their children's teachers, as well as the staff, and share in the educational experience of their child.

The reciprocal relationship that must be in place between schools and Hispanic parents cannot be overemphasized. Schools must make every effort to encourage these parents to visit the school, attend parent-teacher meetings, come to school plays, and other events, so as to make the educational atmosphere welcoming to the entire family. Parents must also overcome whatever fears or anxieties they may have had regarding school, based upon their own past experiences. Many parents are haunted by their own past academic failures and thus are less likely to fully participate in school ventures or to talk to teachers based upon their internalized, or culture-bound, view of education. As Rathvon (1996) explains,

> ". . . for parents who have been unable to work through negative feelings about their own school years, the child's academic experiences trigger troubling memories and emotions. . . . Parents may have painful memories associated with certain grades, teachers, subjects, or school situations such as taking tests or performing in front of their classmates. But the feelings and memories that are most likely to interfere with their efforts to encourage their child's achievement are related to their own parents' interactions with them about school. As the child progresses through school, his experiences reactivate those disturbing memories and feelings. To ward off their painful emotions parents may try to deny them." (p. 87)

It is perhaps the students who feel little encouragement and validation from their parents as well as little attention from the teachers at school, who are at most risk of a low level of academic resilience, and thus more likely to drop out of school. Nevertheless, teachers and counselors in inner-city schools with a high Latino population must do their part to provide a safety net *on the assumption that perhaps an at-risk student may not have an adequate support system at home.*

This is why teachers must remain in close contact with the students' homes and caregivers, and whenever necessary to call the parents, personally, to schedule meetings, or to talk about the students' performance. There is a well-known danger that if a teacher sends a slip or letter home with a student, he or she may "lose" it, or forge the signature of the parents, and the parents remain uninformed of important school developments. This is why important school information, if it is to be sent in letterform at all, should be mailed directly to the parents. This is especially crucial if the student is earning low marks and is hiding this fact, perhaps out of shame, embarrassment or worst of all, fear, from his parents.

Yet another protective factor that was identified by Gutman and Midgley (2000), was a sense of belonging, which students must feel in order to have a sense of affiliation with their school and all its extracurricular activities. They reference Goodenow and Grady (1994), who discovered that ". . . a sense of school belonging was significantly associated with the school motivation and engagement of low-income African American and Hispanics early adolescents." (p. 227) Along those lines, Comer (1980) found that "Parents' interest in, and support of, their children's school help reinforce students' feelings of school belonging and their identification with teachers and other school personnel." (As referenced by Gutman and Midgley, 2000, p. 228).

Additionally, Wayman (2002), suggests that greater attention should be given to the students that are less involved with their school. These students may find themselves facing lower expectations from both teachers and counselors. However, Buriel (1983); Fine & Rosenberg (1983) found that students who are ". . . less involved in school often face reduced attention and expectations." (As referenced by Wayman, 2002, p. 176) Wayman further points out to the fact that such students may benefit from hearing such comments as "You can finish high school," or, "We expect you to finish high school." (p. 176)

A final point must be made with reference to Latino culture. According to Midgley and Arunkumar (1996), "African American students may want to disassociate themselves from schools that reflect the predominant White, middle-class ideology." (p. 435) This quotation is important, for if Latino students are to succeed in school, they must not fall prey to this same phenomenon. Hispanic parents must do all they can to make sure that their children are as assimilated as possible to the culture of the school. Otherwise, this will create, and most likely has created, an oppositional orientation in the students away from the culture of the school. As Midgley and Arunkumar stated,

> "For [minority] students who are oriented to demonstrating their ability, [opposition to the school culture] may provide a dilemma. How does one demonstrate ability and dissociate from school at the same time? Handicapping may provide a solution. By using these strategies, ego-oriented [minority students] can demonstrate to others that they are able and at the same time reject the mainstream culture." (p. 435)

Latino students can be saved this quagmire if their parents make an effort to teach them English at an early age and give them the tools they need to succeed in school. Otherwise, if the parents raise them to be heavily traditional, these students might feel lost and torn between the culture of their home and the culture of the school. In college-age students, this may not present much of a problem. However, it can be a big problem if their child is in the early grades, and his or her English, reading, or writing skills are not up to par. Latino parents will not be able to help the child with homework, or communicate with their child's teachers due their inability to communicate in English.

Additionally, a sense of *belonging* is crucial for a child to succeed in school. Thus, parents must encourage their child to embrace the culture of the school over and above the embrace of the ethnic culture at home. This is not at all a recommendation for parents to deny their children their right to enjoy their ethnic heritage. Rather, this is a call for parents to encourage their children to be included, wholeheartedly, in the school culture, even if it has a different value system than the parents' ethnic culture. This will help a child to develop one of the necessary ingredients, belonging, which is a critical component of academic resilience. What is clearly evident is that no single factor contributes toward the development, promotion, and sustenance of academic resilience; many factors combine and interact with one another, symbiotically, to create and sustain it.

Chapter Twelve

Concluding Thoughts & My Story

At this time in American history, Latin Americans are poised to make major strides in education and in the workforce. Latinos have a vibrant, energetic approach to life, and if this energy can be channeled carefully enough, then Latinos can make a positive and lasting impact on the American scene. It is precisely this energy and vibrancy that has allowed the Latin American culture to survive intact for hundreds of years. Latinos have survived almost every major catastrophe, and yet their spirit is left unbroken. It is this indomitable spirit in the Latin American culture that is special. Inside this spirit lies the core, the absolute center of the Hispanic mind, which no earthquake, no flood, no hurricane, or other earthly disaster can destroy. The aim of this book is to tap into that core and awaken within it the sense of wonder and growth that has allowed all human societies to flourish and blossom.

Spanish was the only language familiar to me during my boyhood. My parents, out of habit, spoke to me in their native language, and that was the language my ears first heard. The situation was relatively benign. However, when I began elementary school, all my teachers were Irish Catholic Nuns. "Burrito" was most likely the extent of the Spanish they knew. One of my former classmates told me, decades later, that she also did not know a word of English when we began the first grade together. We were two little Mexican Americans, age 6, surrounded by an ocean of Irish Catholicism. No one spoke my language. Nor should anyone have done so. The year was 1979. This was, ipso facto, an English language immersion program. Even before the bilingual debate ever started, the classes we were in were literal "sink or swim" models of English language instruction. We were inundated with English for 6 hours a day, five days a week. However, my parents continued to be speak to me in Spanish. This is where my trouble began. Instruction in English was being given in the classroom, but at home, Spanish was still being promoted. My proficiency in English was not developing as a matter of course. Consequently, I was having trouble keeping up with the material in class. My memory is still clear in recalling how my classmates would get up from their seats to turn in their completed assignments, while my assignments were still far from completed. By the second grade, my second grade teacher had a conference with my mother. She suggested that either my parents teach me English, or we should return to Mexico. The choice was theirs. This became a pivotal point in my parochial education. In their wisdom, my parents changed their linguistic practices 180 degrees, and began to speak to me only in English. Fortunately, my parents were both bilingual and very proficient in the English language. Both my parents had acquired the English language in their late teens, not long after having arrived in the United States from Mexico.

Slowly but surely, my proficiency in English began to improve. All my conversations at home were in English. All music, books, television and printed media at home were likewise in English. But the progress was slow going. By the eighth grade, my English skills were in good shape. My vocabulary in English had expanded to the point where I could show off my ability to pronounce the really long words that even my Anglo classmates could not pronounce. And they had known English their whole lives! At that time, my parents were also providing me with private tutoring at home in a wide range of subjects. This rounded out my formal education from school. These lessons included instruction in drawing, karate, swimming, math, racquetball, tennis, and the flute. This went a long way in helping me to expand my intellectual as well as athletic skills. My parents were helping me to become a true Renaissance man. This is where Latino parents can do much to improve their children's education: supplying their children with enriching extracurricular activities.

Some years later, my parents arranged for me to receive home schooling during my high school years. It was felt that this would shield me from certain undesirable aspects of high school life during those years. This of course brings up controversy over whether a teenager who is home schooled acquires the necessary social skills and experiences that are so much a part of adolescence. Nevertheless, after completing a few years of home schooling, I enrolled in an Adult Education School. After completing the requisite classes, I received my General Education Development (GED) diploma in 1992. In the spring of 1993, I enrolled at Long Beach City College. This was a huge step for me and for my parents. One of my first memories of college is walking the campus at night, close to Christmas 1992, and thinking that college would be a strange, foreign world to me. College. The very idea of it scared me. The campus seemed like a forbidding labyrinth. The school where I earned by GED had been just a few classrooms in an elementary school that was converted into a school for adults.

Nevertheless, my studies began at Long Beach City College. At first, my course load was light. It felt so odd to be walking the halls of a college, a junior college at that. Two years later, during the summer of 1995, and after having completed all of my general education classes, my interests had not focused upon a major. So, at my parents' suggestion, my college classes were put on hold, while I studied business and accounting classes at the Southeast campus of the Regional Occupational Program (ROP) School for adults. This is a school for adults who are seeking employment in the trades, such as accounting, or nursing, or auto-mechanics. The school was tuition free. The few textbooks that were required were the only expense. I studied accounting and business software for one year, only to decide that accounting was not interesting to me. Psychology was, and had always been, my real interest. I had read several "pop-psychology" books during my adolescence in an attempt to understand myself better, and was thus very familiar and comfortable with the subject. So, upon my return to Long Beach City College in the fall semester of 1996, my major in psychology was declared, at last.

This is when my course load became heavy. I took my Lower Division classes for my major. At the same time, I applied to California State University, Long Beach (CSULB), and was accepted. My coursework there began during the spring term of 1997. This is when my abilities as a college student really began to skyrocket. Semester after semester, my high grades earned my placement on the President's List. The only "B" I earned at CSULB was in golf!

By the end of my first year at CSULB, in December 1997, I was inducted into two honor societies, Psi Chi, the National Honor Society of Psychology students, and Golden Key, which is an interdisciplinary society that honors the top students from all academic majors. My induction into Psi Chi occurred aboard the Queen Mary, in the Port of Long Beach. That was a big deal for me, as it was for my fellow psychology upperclassmen. The banquet hall was beautifully appointed with Christmas decorations. Then, in April 26, 1998, I got inducted into another honor society, Phi Kappa Phi. Phi Kappa Phi was a real high moment for me personally. Only the top 5 percent of the university were inducted. The Phi Kappa Phi ceremony meant more to me than the actual commencement ceremony that later took place at the end of the spring semester in 1998. Even though I took part in the commencement ceremony, there were still units that needed to be completed in order for me to graduate. So, I took an Anthropology class at Cerritos College. The professor who taught the class later took some of his former students to Mexico to explore the ruins and the native cultures. I paid my fee and joined the expedition. That trip did more to reacquaint me with my Mexican roots than anything else since. There were other elements that made the trip memorable. When we arrived in Mexico City in July of that summer in 1998, the tour director that was hired to be our guide all throughout the trip greeted our group at the airport. She was 25, and ravishing. Mexican beauty and intelligence personified. She sported shoulder-length dark brown hair, almond-shaped eyes, and a Continental view of life. Her philosophies had been shaped and molded by her elite upbringing, her travels to Europe, and her completed education at the University of Mexico City. Her views about life fascinated me. She smoked, which gave her voice a deep, sultry pitch. She took a liking to me. We ended up having a steamy, if secret, sexual fling throughout the length of the two-week trip. She would show me the key with her room number etched on it under the table at dinner. Late at night, she would receive me in her room at whatever hotel we had stayed. Needless to say, there were many elements that made my trip a personal journey of lifetime. I still reminisce a lot about that voyage.

Some time after returning from Mexico, while reading Peterson's Guide to Graduate Schools at the beach, a school caught my eye: The University of La Verne, near Pomona, California. As compared with the other graduate schools, La Verne seemed relatively small, and cheap. Additionally, it was a private school and the general consensus was that a private graduate school would be preferable to a public university. So, I applied for admissions for their graduate program in Counseling, and attended the orientation one calm autumn day in October 1998. It was love at first sight. The autumn leaves were dropping around the campus, giving it a very New England feel to it. It seemed so conservative and formal. Not at all like the surfer culture one observes on the campus at CSULB. Deep down, however, I will always carry the surfer campus culture of CSULB inside me, as my two years there were very special.

In the fall semester of 1998, I took my last semester of coursework at CSULB. It was the most demanding set of final exams of my entire senior year of college. As far as grueling coursework was concerned, they were saving the best for last! However, I finished with a bang, receiving an "A" in each of the classes. It was over. Later my *real* bachelor's degree arrived in the mail, not the fake one that undergraduates hold during their commencement ceremony. On it was the graduation rank of Cum Laude, which is second to the highest graduating rank, Magna Cum Laude. I was 25 years old.

So, after getting accepted to the master's program at the University of La Verne, my graduate studies began in the summer of 1999. At first, my classmates and I were alarmed at the difficulty of the material and the strict manner in which it was being demanded of us. There was a new Chair of the Master's Program, Errol Moultrie, Ph.D., a man for whom I cannot state enough praise. He has long since left the program. Yet, when my classmates and I first got to know him, and vice versa, he just seemed, by first impressions, very stern. Very strict. Severe. There were reports of female students leaving his office in tears after trying to contest a grade. Yet, as we all got to know him, and the idea of a university mutiny no longer seemed feasible (we seriously entertained the notion of complaining formally to the Dean). We began to soften toward him and he likewise softened his approach to us. We began to like him. He, in turn, began to display to us how much he believed in us. In the end, he was showing us a kind of "tough love."

Writing my thesis was quite an ordeal. Night after night, my midnight oil burned as I kept writing, editing, and amending the paper. My father aided my efforts tirelessly by reading, proofreading, and editing the thesis. Were it not for his assistance, I doubt that I would have made it through that dark period. He helped me hone my words and thoughts so that the finish product was as smooth and seamless as possible. The frightening part came on the evening when all of us had to present and defend our theses. My father showed up at the university the night I defended my thesis. We were all quite anxious that night. Yet, after a few revisions, Dr. Moultrie approved the paper, and my program was thus completed. When all of us took part in the commencement ceremony in 2002, it was a very emotional event. There were already rumors that Dr. Moultrie was leaving the university. When he finally left, we were quite sad. Yet, we had made it. My personal journey had come the full route: from a little six year old boy who could barely speak any English, to a twenty nine year old in possession of a master's degree.

After doing some minor paid research for a faculty member at the University of La Verne, I joined the Peace Corps. My first choice was Europe, and my wish was granted. My group flew off to the Republic of Moldova, in Eastern Europe, not more than one week after my commencement in late May of 2002. The first leg of the trip started in Atlanta, Georgia. This was to be our "Staging," or first stage, when all of us would first meet and attend a few seminars before flying off to Frankfurt, Germany, our first and only layover. From Germany, we left for Moldova. The Republic of Moldova is one of the newer countries formed after the dissolution of the Soviet Union. It lies between Romania and Ukraine. My assigned duty at post was to be an English as a Second Language (ESL) instructor, while the other volunteers, sixty-six in total, were trained to serve in health or agricultural fields of work. After three grueling months of training, and intense language training in Romanian, we were sworn in. The swearing in ceremony took place in a beautiful and very spacious auditorium in a government palace in the capital city, Chisinau. The ceremony had all the pomp of any federal program, with all of us raising our right hands and swearing allegiance to the Constitution of the United States, etc. I was very impressed by it all.

The ESL volunteers, including myself, spent the entire three months of training living in a town called Mitoc. It was difficult and trying, to be sure. The weather was hot and humid. The villages to me had all the rustic appeal of a Hollywood movie. But, nevertheless, it was difficult being away from home. After the three months of training concluded, and after the subsequent swearing in ceremony, were we all sent to our *permanent* sites. These towns were where we would be volunteering our services for the entire tour of two years. These sites were all completely different from the villages and towns that we had trained in. In addition, we had lived with host families for the entire duration of our training, and had become more or less used to the families that we had lived with. Some of the volunteers had become quite attached to their host families. When the day came that we were to be relocated to our permanent villages, many volunteers became tearful. We had moved back to the capital city for only two days for the swearing in ceremony, and then moved to our permanent posts. My site was called Chimislia. It lies south of the capital city, Chisinau. I arrived and settled in with my new host family, who spoke more Russian than they did Romanian. Communication was thus a problem. In addition, learning the Romanian language was very difficult for me during those three grueling months.

There were a few pleasurable distractions. My host family's cuisine appealed to me. The vineyard in their front yard gave their home a very rustic appeal. There were other things that I had become used to while living in Moldova. For instance, my laundry was washed by hand in the backyards of my host families' homes. At the home where I was training, hot water for bathing had to be heated on a stove first, then transported by bucket out to the outdoor shower stall. I had to climb a ladder, with a huge bucket filled with boiling water in hand, and pour it into the basin at the top of the structure. This would allow the hot water to collect and then rain down on me as I showered. It was taken for granted that my host family in Mitoc would always allow me to have a ready supply of hot water for bathing, but there were a couple of times when my hair and my eyes were covered with shampoo suds, and all of a sudden the water would stop flowing. That was life in Moldova. That's not to say it was all hardship. The Moldovans love to throw parties. I attended more than a few parties where the table was overflowing with food and wine and vodka, and the music and dancing continued until late into the night. After centuries and hardship, ethnic Moldovans have ingrained in them a love of enjoying the moment. Why not party today? You never know what hardships tomorrow may bring. This is very reminiscent to the love of throwing *fiestas* seen in the Hispanic community.

In the end, however, my homesickness was too strong for me to continue my venture in Moldova. I was to be the only American at my permanent post, or town, and that seemed too lonesome for me. It would have been nice to have at least another Peace Corps volunteer with whom to share time and conversations. So, I terminated my service and came home. It was an emotional return for me. This was my first protracted period of time away from home, and it was the furthest of my sojourns. Yet, my soul was enriched by the experience. Additionally, my Peace Corps adventure allowed me to feel what it must be like for a foreigner to come to the United States and experience life as an "outsider." It was my turn to be foreigner living in a strange new world. Their language, music, currency and overall *modus vivendi* were all so foreign to me.

My Peace Corps experience allowed me to become empathic towards people who come live in United States. It must be an overwhelming experience. One can only imagine how hard it is for those foreigners whose native language is not based on the Roman alphabet, like Asians, to learn not only a new language, but to learn a new alphabet as well. This is why my convictions of assimilation and cultural integration are always tempered and softened by my experiences in Europe. One has to always place oneself in the other person's shoes, and imagine what an experience feels like for the person who is the target of one's criticism. This is the art of being empathic. I have developed a great deal of empathy for the scores of immigrants who come to the shores of the United States every year. Having to be torn away from one's family, loved ones, spouses, roots, and houses of worship must be very traumatic. Psychologists have done studies that point out that the most traumatic event for a person, second only to losing a loved one, is moving to a new area. They were only referring to people moving to a new area within the United States! Just imagine having to flee a country that is war-torn, or being on board one of the freighters that has brought so many of the Chinese to the coast of San Francisco. These unfortunate souls no doubt suffer psychological trauma for life. These people embody courage, tenacity and strength of spirit. This also does not even take into account the countless others who have lost their lives in the attempt to reach the shores of America. This book is ultimately dedicated to all those who have perished in the attempt to reach Lady Liberty.

In the end, each one of us must find within ourselves the inner strength, convictions, and spiritual truths that can guide us to be our best. Over the last two centuries, the American flag has been stitched together by countless threads. Each thread represents each of the brave men, women, and children who have decided to better their lives by becoming an American. They made the choice. They made the voyage. They made a difference. My challenge to the reader is to add his or her own special weave into the American flag. Furthermore, the reader must understand that perseverance and an undying belief in oneself are all that is necessary to triumph over difficult obstacles in life.

Let me illustrate another fine example of a family whose children beat the odds: the Perez family. On Friday, May 14, 2004, Stuart Silverstein, a writer for *The Los Angeles Times*, published a story about a family that lives in Pacoima, in Southern California. The area is predominantly Hispanic, and poor. Yet, Samuel and Maria Elena Perez, both immigrants from Mexico, were able to put their 11 children through college. Furthermore, neither Samuel nor Maria Elena advanced beyond the sixth grade. Yet, because of the high standards the Perez parents set for their children, they are enjoying something truly extraordinary. Their youngest daughter, Maria Elena Perez, 21, just graduated from the University of Southern California. The family also cite tight supervision over the children as they were growing up as important in their staying on the right track. Financially, the 11 Perez offspring received Pell and Cal Grants both of which are federal monies awarded to students demonstrating financial duress. Some also earned scholarships from the University of Southern California. They also held jobs while earning their degrees and took advantage of student loans. Culturally, the Perez family ignored the cultural taboo of sending young people, especially females, to live away from home. This is something many Latino families are unwilling to do. Yet, look at what can be accomplished when children are sent away to college!

Let this twenty first century be the century for Latinos. It is time for Latin Americans to claim their right to the American Dream. Hispanics deserve a better role for themselves in education, and the occupational world. Latinos have the ability. They don't have to go looking for ways to be successful. . .

All they have to do is look inside.

Bibliography

Arfaniarromo, Albert. "Toward a psychosocial and sociocultural understanding of achievement motivation among Latino gang members in U.S. schools." *Journal of Instructional Psychology* 28, no.3 (2001): 123–31. http://www.questia.com.

Barnes, Julian E. "Unequal Education." *U.S. News & World Report*, March 2004, 66–75.

Berne, Eric. *Games People Play: The Basic Handbook of Transactional Analysis.* New York: Ballantine Books, 1964.

Bernhard, Judith K., et.al. "Latin Americans in a Canadian primary school: perspectives of parents, teachers, and children on cultural identity and academic achievement." *Canadian Journal of Regional Science* 20, no. 1–2 (1997): 217–36. http://www.questia.com.

Braxton, Richard J. "Culture, family and Chinese and Korean American student achievement: An examination of student factors that affect student outcomes." *College Student Journal* 33, no. 2 (1999): 250–56. http://www.questia.com.

Chavez, Linda and Lyons, James J. "Q: is bilingual education failing to help America's schoolchildren?" *Insight on the News* 12, no. 21 (1996): 24–27. http://www.questia.com.

Chavez, Linda. "Our Hispanic predicament: Lack of U.S. assimilation despite economic progress." *Commentary Magazine*, August 25, 2005, 47–50. http://commentarymagazine.com.

Covina-Valley Unified School District. "Ways to Help Your Child Succeed in School." Lark Ellen Elementary School. http://www.cvusd.k.12.ca.us/Lark_Ellend/mrp/success_in_school.html

DeBlassie, Richard R. "Education of Hispanic youth: a cultural lag." *Adolescence* 31, no. 131 (1996): 205–211. http://www.questia.com.

Espinoza-Herold, Mariella. *Issues in Latino education: race, school culture, and the politics of academic success.* Boston: Allyn and Bacon, 2003.

Figueroa, Richard A. "Special education for Latino students in the United States." *Bilingual Review* (1999) 147–56. http://www.questia.com.

Barone, Michael and Fonte, John. "Does America have an assimilation problem?" *The American Enterprise* (2000): 1–9. http://findarticles.com.

Fischer, Judith L., Munsch, Joyce and Pidcock, Boyd W. "Family, personality, and social risk factors impacting the retention rates of first-year Hispanic and Anglo college students." *Adolescence* 36, no. 144 (2001): 803–14. http://www.questia.com.

Gutman, Leslie M. and Midgely, Carol. "The role of protective factors in supporting the academic achievement of poor African American Students during the middle school transition." *Journal of Youth and Adolescence* 29, no. 2 (2000): 223–46. http://www.questia.com.

Hanson, Victor D. *Mexifornia: A State of Becoming*. San Francisco: Encounter Books, 2003.

Huntington, Samuel P. "The Hispanic Challenge." *Foreign Policy*, March 2004, 30–45.

Huntington, Samuel P. *Who Are We? The Challenges to America's National Identity*. New York: Simon & Schuster, 2004.

Karo, Aaron. *Ruminations on College Life*. New York: Simon & Schuster, 2002.

Martin, Andrew. "Motivation and academic resilience: Developing a model for student enhancement." *Australian Journal of Education* 46, no. 1(2002): 34–45. http://www.questia.com.

Midgley, Carol and Arunkumar, Revathy. "If I don't do well tomorrow, there's a reason: predictors of adolescents' use of academic self-handicapping strategies." *Journal of Educational Psychology*. 88, no. 3 (1996): 431–37. http://www.questia.com.

Nunez-Janes, Mariela. "Bilingual education and identity debates in New Mexico: constructing and contesting nationalism and ethnicity." *Journal of the Southwest* 44, no.1 (2002): 61–72. http://www.questia.com.

Perlmann, Joel. "Are the children of today's immigrants making it?" *The Public Interest* (1998): 1–15. http://findarticles.com.

Reese, Leslie. "Morality and identity in Mexican immigrant parents' vision of the future." *Journal of Ethnic and Migration studies* (2001): 1–14. http://highbeam.com.

Raspberry, William. "The Education Gap." *The Record*, October 12, 2003. http://highbeam.com.

Robinson, Leroy. "Education does matter: parents should expect their children to do better in school." *Indianapolis Recorder*, November 7, 2003. http://highbeam.com.

Rossell, Christine H. "The near end of bilingual: Prop 227 was supposed to eliminate bilingual education from California's schools. For the most part, it succeeded—and student performance is climbing slowly upward." *Education Next*, September 22, 2003, 1–6. http://highbeam.com.

Silverstein, Stuart. "Dedication Paying Off in Degrees." *Los Angeles Times*, May 14, 2004, sec. B.

Siwatu, Kamau O. "Promoting academic persistence in African American and Latino high school students: The educational navigation skills seminar." *High School Journal* (2003): 1–10. http://highbeam.com.

Stockstill, Mason. "Remittances Spawn Mini-Industry in the United States." *Los Angeles Newspaper Group*, July 11, 2005. http://lang.dailybulletin.com/socal/beyond-borders/part_2/p2_day2_remitt.asp

Suarez-Orozco, Marcelo .M. "Everything you ever wanted to know about assimilation but were afraid to ask." *Daedalus* 129, no. 4 (2000): 1–14. http://www.questia.com.

Swain, Carol M. *The New White Nationalism in America: Its Challenge to Integration.* Cambridge: Cambridge University Press, 2002.

Thernstrom, Abigail and Stephan Thernstrom. *No Excuses: Closing the Racial Gap in Learning.* New York: Simon & Schuster, 2003.

Valladares, Mayra R. "The Dropouts." *Hispanic*, December 1, 2002, 1–9. http://highbeam.com.

Valladares, Mayra R. "Rising to the Challenge." *Hispanic*, July 1, 2003, 26–30. http://highbeam.com.

Valladares, Mayra R. "Getting Past Enrollment." *Hispanic*, May 2003, 30–34.

Valverde, Leonard, ed. *The Latino Student's Guide to College Success.* Westport: Greenwood Press, 2002.

Wayman, Jeffrey C. "The utility of educational resilience for studying degree attainment in school dropout." *The Journal of Educational Research.* 95, no. 3 (2002): 167–84. http://www.questia.com.

Zhou, Min. "Growing up American: The challenge confronting immigrant children and children of immigrants." *Annual Review of Sociology* 23 (1997): 63–86. http://www.questia.com.

Index

About the Author

Ernesto Caravantes grew up in Lakewood, California. He faced certain challenges as the only son of Mexican immigrant parents. From his struggles to learn English as a first-grader, and sitting in remedial English classes as a sixth grader, to his completion of a master's degree, his life has been marked by a steady uphill progression of learning new abilities and honing his skills. He has steadily striven to grow and expand all areas of his life. Now he wishes to share his experiences with his readers. His early experiences visiting the meat markets of Los Angeles with his parents showed him firsthand how beleaguered and unassimilated the Hispanic population had become in California. He saw firsthand how Latino immigrants were living in Los Angeles as if they were still living in their native country. In *Clipping Their Own Wings*, Mr. Caravantes shows the reader how the Latino culture is the culprit for Hispanic underachievement in the United States. But there is a ray of hope, however. He pinpoints exactly how Hispanics can advance themselves in society, without necessarily having to give up the beauty, spirit and lyricism that have given so much richness to Latin American culture.

Mr. Caravantes enjoys swimming, practicing the Martial Arts, writing, and spending time near the ocean. He currently resides in Southern California. He can be reached at: csulb1998@hotmail.com.

www.ingramcontent.com/pod-product-compliance
Lightning Source LLC
Chambersburg PA
CBHW021821270326
41932CB00007B/280